The French Revolution Confronts Pius VI

Other Books of Interest from St. Augustine's Press

Daniele Lorenzini, *Jacques Maritain and Human Rights: Totalitarianism, Anti-Semitism and Democracy (1936–1951)*

Edward A. Goerner, *Peter and Caesar: The Catholic Church and Political Authority*

Edward Feser, *The Last Superstition: A Refutation of the New Atheism*

Edward Feser, *Neo-Scholastic Essays*

Gerard V. Bradley, *Unquiet Americans*

Christopher Kaczor, *The Gospel of Happiness: How Secular Psychology Points to the Wisdom of Christian Practice*

James V. Schall, *At a Breezy Time of Day: Selected Schall Interviews on Just about Everything*

James V. Schall, *The Praise of 'Sons of Bitches': On the Worship of God by Fallen Men*

James V. Schall, *The Regensburg Lecture*

Kenneth D. Whitehead (editor), *After 40 Years: Vatican Council II's Diverse Legacy*

Joseph Bottum, *The Decline of the Novel*

Étienne Gilson, *Theology and the Cartesian Doctrine of Freedom*

Josef Kleutgen, S.J., *Pre-Modern Philosophy Defended*

Philippe Bénéton, *The Kingdom Suffereth Violence*

Ernest A. Fortin, A.A., *Christianity and Philosophical Culture in the Fifth Century: The Controversy about the Human Soul in the West*

Peter Kreeft, *Ecumenical Jihad*

Peter Kreeft, *Socrates' Children: The 100 Greatest Philosophers*

Josef Pieper, *The Christian Idea of Man*

Josef Pieper and Heinz Raskop, *What Catholics Believe*

Karl Rahner, *Encounters with Silence*

René Girard, *A Theater of Envy: William Shakespeare*

The French Revolution Confronts Pius VI

Volume I: His Writings to Louis XVI, French Cardinals, Bishops, the National Assembly, and the People of France, with Special Emphasis on the Civil Constitution of the Clergy

Pope Pius VI

Translated with Commentary by Jeffrey J. Langan

St. Augustine's Press
South Bend, Indiana

Manufactured in the United States of America.

1 2 3 4 5 6 26 25 24 23 22 21 20

Library of Congress Cataloging-in-Publication Data

Pius VI, Pope, 1717–1799.
[Collection generale des brefs et instructions de N.S.P. le Pape Pie VI. relatifs à la Révolution françoise. English]
The French Revolution confronts Pius VI / translation and commentary by Jeffrey J. Langan.
volumes cm
Originally compiled and published in French by M.N.S. Guillon in two volumes in 1798 and 1790 respectively; the first volume contained the speeches and letters of Pius VI with respect to the events leading up to the passage and implementation of Civil Constitution of the Clergy; the second volume contained letters revealing the Pope's actions up to his death in 1799.
ISBN 978-1-58731-259-5 (clothbound: alkaline paper) 1. France – History – Revolution, 1789–1799 – Religious aspects – Sources. 2. Pius VI, Pope, 1717–1799 – Archives. 3. Catholic Church – France – History – 18th century – Sources. 4. Church and state – France – History – 18th century – Sources. I. Langan, Jeffrey, 1970– II. Guillon, M.-N.-S. (Marie-Nicolas-Silvestre), 1760–1847. III. Catholic Church. Pope (1775–1799: Pius VI) IV. Title.
DC158.2.P55 2013
944.04 – dc23 2013040169

∞ The paper used in this publication meets the minimum requirements of the American National Standard for Information Sciences - Permanence of Paper for Printed Materials, ANSI Z39.48-1984.

St. Augustine's Press
www.staugustine.net

Commentary and Introduction

"I have no fear in now admitting here, what I have only partly gestured at earlier, that the Civil Constitution of the Clergy passed by the Constituent Assembly, was perhaps the greatest political error of that Assembly. This is true, even if we separate the act from the terrible crimes that followed from the act."[1] These words, taken from the *Mémoires du Prince de Talleyrand* and published more than twenty years after his death in 1838, provide us with perhaps the greatest reason for translating and commenting on the speeches of Pius VI during the French Revolution, especially the speeches that reveal his attitude toward, and reaction to, the Civil Constitution of the Clergy. In his *Mémoires*, Talleyrand admits that the essential point that both Pius VI, and after him, Pius VII, defended was the independence of the Church to appoint her own bishops. By defending this freedom, they were defending the rights of the Church to remain independent from all political orders so that she could impartially exercise her power and influence. It is not reasonable, Talleyrand saw toward the end of his life, to expect the Church to give up her freedom and go back to the Catacombs.

The drama of Pius VII versus Napoleon is perhaps better known to historians and students of the time, not as well known, and yet, by Talleyrand's admission, equally important, is the error of the Assembly in passing the Civil Constitution of the Clergy in the first place, as well as Pius VI's attempts to prevent them from making that error while articulating the nature of the error. Inasmuch as historians have dealt with the actions of Pius VI during the revolution, they seem to take the position that he, in fact, did too little too late to oppose the Civil Constitution.

1 Talleyrand, *Mémoires du Prince de Talleyrand* (Paris: Les Éditions Henri Javal, 1953), 2:110.

One cliché, which seems to go back to the 1790s, is that Pius was more interested in draining the marshes around the Vatican than he was concerned about the affairs in France.

The observations from the *Mémoires* of Talleyrand suggest otherwise. And so, it would be important, if we wanted to flesh out his ideas, to look at the evidence available to us in order to determine the thought of Pius VI with respect to the Civil Constitution and his attempts to prevent its passage. His opposition to the greatest error of the Assembly would be historically significant, especially if he could articulate a rationale for defending the freedom of the Church.

M.N.S Guillon thought that Pius VI provided such a defense. And so, as early as 1798 he published a volume containing the speeches and letters of Pius VI with respect to the events leading up to the passage and implementation of Civil Constitution of the Clergy, the letters translated in this volume. He published a second volume of letters in 1790, revealing the Pope's actions up to his death in 1799. However, Guillon's volumes have never been given the historical influence that he hoped they would have. Due to the ransacking of libraries by revolutionary armies, the vicissitudes of nineteenth century French politics, and the reticence of the largely Marxist-dominated historiography on the French Revolution, the collection of Guillon never became a significant part of the historical debate. As of the 1990s, there were no copies of Guillon's works in the public libraries of Paris. Now, with the help of the internet, the original volumes are available on Google Books, but they have not been translated into English. And so, we have before us an instance in which the internet might help advance the English-speaking world's understanding of history.

If we turn to the writings themselves, we do not find someone who was practically indifferent to the events of the Revolution. To the contrary, we see someone who recognizes all too well the behavior of the revolutionaries and where their actions are headed. The Pope was not a delusionary renaissance Pope, as some historiography has made him out to be. To the contrary, he was a competent diplomat who knew how to exercise statesmanship in the midst of circumstances in which he realized he had little or no political power. He could do this because he was a student of history. His knowledge of the past, as well as his knowledge of moral principles, led him to understand the limited power of the Papacy in revolutionary times. He understood that in fact there were elements in the Revolution that were directly hostile to the Catholic Church and that the Church had to prepare to suffer during revolutionary times.

Following his knowledge of the past, Pius VI could reason that just as kings of old had attempted to control religion so as to consolidate their political power, so too the new regime had attempted to control religion to consolidate the power of a democratic empire. The Pope, as the Church had always done, resisted such efforts as he could, by teaching and by appeals to reason. In resisting such efforts, the Pope accepted the political changes brought about in France during the Revolution.

At the same time that Pius VI accepted political change, he critiqued the philosophical ethos upon which those political changes were founded. In critiquing this ethos, we see a basic structure emerging that has governed church-state relations and the conflict between the Enlightenment and the Church that persists until our own day. Finally, at the end of his life, when imprisoned, he understood this contradiction as God's providence working itself out in history. He did not see his imprisonment as a personal tragedy. It brought him joy. In these circumstances, his concern was still to care for the souls for whom he was responsible.

In order to fully understand the letters in this Volume, we can divide them into two parts: 1. the actions of the revolutionaries before debating and implementing the Civil Constitution of the Clergy, 1789–March 1790; 2. drafting, passing and implementing the Civil Constitution of the Clergy, April 1790 – 1791.

The period from 1789 to April 1790 can be characterized as a series of not necessarily connected events in which the Assembly was attempting to resolve political and religious problems. The controversy over religion began in 1789. On 11 August 1789 the Assembly abolished tithing. On 2 November of the same year, it nationalized Church property. The Assembly did not make clear at this time its ultimate objectives. It did send a message to Rome that it was appropriating Church land in case of a national emergency.[2] On 13 February 1790 events became more dramatic.

2 Ludwig Pastor, *The History of the Popes From the Close of the Middle Ages*, trans. EF Peeler, (St. Louis: Herder Book Co., 1953), XL: 118-19.

The Assembly forbade the taking of monastic vows and banned religious orders except those that were involved in teaching or care of the sick. It also took more aggressive measures with respect to Church property on 19 April, transferring all Church property to the state.

With this first period over, the Assembly committed itself to a more systematic approach that involved nothing less than re-organizing the entire Catholic Church in France. This process resulted in the drafting and implementation of the Civil Constitution of the Clergy as well as the creation of a schismatic Church in France. On 6 February 1790 the Assembly established a committee to draft a constitution for the clergy of France. The committee submitted its work for debate before the Assembly, and by 12 July the Constitution had been passed. Provisions of the Constitution included reducing the number of bishops in France from 135 to 83, subjecting them along with priests to democratic elections, and requiring voters, whether Catholic, Protestant, or Jewish, to take an oath of loyalty to the Constitution.

While the Assembly passed the measure, Louis XVI hesitated approving it. In his mind, he would have liked to approve the measure and retain good favor with the Pope. As of July 1790 he still had the power to put his pen to a law once passed. He indicated to the Assembly that he would like to consult with Rome before signing the measure. In the final third of 1790 he exchanged several letters with Pius VI on the subject of the Constitution.

As the King and the Pope dialogued, events in France intensified. On 10 October 1790 thirty French bishops wrote to Pius VI opining that they would not accept the Constitution on the Clergy. Four bishops dissented. The thirty made their opinions public on 30 October. One cannot be sure if the Assembly acted in response to events or to their own principles, but on 27 October it passed a law that not only required electors to take an oath of loyalty to the new Civil Constitution, but it required all priests and bishops to make a similar oath. Louis XVI, after much hesitation, finally signed the full Civil Constitution of the Clergy into law on 26 December 1790, leading to its implementation in January and February 1791.

The Civil Constitution created a schism in the Church in France from 1791 to 1801. The schism was determined by what priests took the oath of loyalty and those who did not take the oath. The oath-takers came to be known as juring priests. Those who failed to take it non-juring or refractory priests. From 1791 to 1795 the refractory priests, and eventually even the juring priests, were subject to various levels of punishments as deviants under the law, which included unpunished violence, exile, imprisonments, and death.

After the events of 1791, the Assembly took more aggressive measures. On 17 August 1792 the Assembly quashed all female religious orders, ordering all nuns to leave their convents by 1 October. The Assembly then dissolved all religious congregations on 18 August. On 26 August they commended all non-juring priests to leave France within a fortnight. By 23 April 1793 the Assembly determined that every refractory priest still in France was to be put to death within twenty-four hours of his conviction.[3] There is more that could be told about the war on Catholics in the Vendee, for example. This war, to be sure, was foremost in Talleyrand's mind when he made his comments about the grave mistake that the Civil Constitution turned out to be.

The letters of Pius VI reveal that he understood the delicate task that faced him as Pope: he lacked any really political leverage. He had to deal with revolutionaries who would spread lies, intercept his letters, write false letters, and, in short, go to violent extremes to eliminate the influence of the Pope. He knew from early on that Louis XVI effectively had lost power. While he preferred monarchy, Pius VI also recognized the autonomy of a nation of establish democratic forms of government, and that such governments also needed to respect the freedom of the Church. Understanding these circumstances, he knew that he had to implement a strategy in which the primary exercise of influence would be by the word of one person to the next. He also recognized that since the revolutionaries would be prone to violence, he had to wait for the right moment to speak clearly about the Civil Constitution. At the very least, reading these letters will reveal a more subtle strategy, but a real strategy, than someone whose public silence simply indicated indifference.

In addition to showing the statesmanship of Pius VI, these letters also reveal the stance that the Pope took with respect to the political

3 Pastor, *The History of the Popes*, 196–202.

philosophies of the eighteenth century. Pius VI saw that the radical thoughts and deeds of the French Revolution were the result of high-level Churchmen and Catholic intellectuals attempting to compromise with the seemingly benign, but in reality insidious, ideas of the Enlightenment. He understood that the logical conclusion of these seemingly benign ideas was a regime based on fear and oppression, or, as Benedict XVI has reminded us, a dictatorship of relativism.

And so, it is the hope of the translator of these letters that they will initiate a new look at the early events of the Revolution, taking into account the thoughts and actions of Pius VI, who represents, as Talleyrand admitted in his *Mémoires*, the institution that understood, and knew how to react to, the biggest mistake that the revolutionaries in France made and that revolutionaries of all times, including our own, are prone to make.

Speech of the Pope in Secret Consistory, 9 March 1790

Venerable Brothers,

We would like to speak to you today about the great anxieties that presently weigh upon us. We feel called to share our concerns with you. It is now universally known and without a doubt that France has fall into a sad state. This vast and flourishing monarchy once held the most important position in Europe. Today, she has now suddenly fallen into an abyss of misery. She approaches ruin due to the actions of some of her own citizens. The revolutionaries' first claimed to establish order in public administration and to reduce public spending. It seemed that these goals were very far from anything that had to do with the responsibilities of our apostolic ministry. But now, out of nowhere, they have gone beyond simply creating a political constitution. They are creating a religion itself, a religion that is meant to be subordinate to and at the service of their political interests.

At the same time, we have heard rumors of violence inspired by these seditious and cruel subjects. Violence and sedition can only end in bloodshed. When we heard of these details, which grow more alarming every day, our first thoughts were to beg for divine mercy for this nation. We call for daily public prayers to be said every day for this end. But you can see that God has not yet heard these prayers. And so, with deepest sorrow, the evil grows and makes progress. We hope that we will never see how far the violence will go.

The Estates General of France have passed decrees that directly attack and destabilize religion. They usurp the rights of the Apostolic See. They violate solemn agreements and treaties. They open up a path for and give greater publicity to evil and false doctrines that infect the writings and books that have recently circulated among the people. Some of the first decrees of the assembly give the impression that each man is free to think as he pleases, especially in religious matters, and to proclaim publically his ideas with impunity. They also claim that every man can only be joined to other men by laws to which he consents. Furthermore, in debating the matter, they have come to think that the Catholic faith should not be the predominant religion, or better yet, that it should not be kept at all in France. Non-Catholics can now hold any military or civil position.

They have also decreed that the state will no longer recognize solemn religious vows. They will encourage all of the members of religious communities of both sexes to leave their convents and monasteries. They have stolen the lands of the Church in the interest of putting them at the service of the nation. They have abolished tithes, which had previously done much good. They have taken the altars and the silver goods from the churches. And now, they are deliberating about what they can seize next.

Now that we have heard about these injustices, can we let them pass in silence? Should we not raise our voice against these unjust decrees that push religion to the brink? Are we going to see an interruption or perhaps even a complete break in relations between the Holy See and the throne of France? If we were to remain silent, we could apply to our silence the words of the prophet Isaiah: "Woe to me, because I have remained silent!"

But the problem we must consider is how best to break the silence. To whom should we speak? Should we call on the bishops? They are stripped of their legitimate authority and struck with terror. They have fled their offices. What about the clergy? They are dispersed and discouraged. They no longer have the right of assembly.

Can we have recourse to the King? His authority has been usurped. He is now subject to the Estates and seems to be forced to assent to all of their decrees. The nation follows, seduced, it seems, by the promise of a false understanding of freedom. It has entrusted itself to the counsel of philosophers who vie among themselves disparaging each other. They have forgotten that Christian doctrine is the most secure foundation for the health of a regime, and that, as Augustine teaches us, the true measure of happiness derives from all citizens giving ready obedience to Kings. Kings who act for the common good are ministers of God and sons of the Church. They protect her, just as they would protect their own mothers, guarding her cause and defending her rights.

We certainly see the difficulties involved in speaking publically, in reminding the people of sound moral principles, in encouraging and strengthening those involved in the conflict. But we know that our voice may soon be ignored. As it is, we see a proliferation of savagery that does not stop at arson, robbery, torture, or massacre. It is a savagery that abandons all humanity. Truth be told, we fear that the people will be more and more stirred up to commit even more, worse crimes. Saint Gregory the Great left us a brilliant document on this topic. Sometimes we should be silent, but we need to study each case to determine when we should be silent and when we should speak. He gave us this rule of conduct: "Let us learn to be discreet, discerning when to be quiet, when it is the right time to open our mouths and what is the right way to be silent once more." Moreover, it is very well known that Athanasius did not only remain silent; he fled Alexandria while his persecutors were in hot pursuit. It was in those circumstances that he wrote: "Do not act so rashly and in such a headstrong way that you tempt the Lord." Saint Gregory Thamaturgus acted in the same way, as did Saint Dionysios of Alexandria. Skilled interpreters of the Scriptures teach the same thing.

It is also true that, for one who has the duty of speaking, his silence must not last forever, but should be kept only until he can break it without danger to himself or others. We have learned by heart the words of Saint Ambrose, who wrote: "David held his peace, not always, nor with everyone, but for a time; and, he did not reply to the taunting of his adversaries, nor to the provocations of sinners."

But since the French people are deaf to anything that we might say, what should we do in the meantime? Certainly, we should be speaking with God. We should open our heart to Him and increase exponentially our petitions to Him! Nevertheless, we count on this discourse of ours to be treated as a witness of the fact that we are aware of how deep are the wounds that have been inflicted on religion, how lively are the attacks against the rights of this Apostolic See; we must make sure that everyone present knows that our silence is not due to indifference or neglect. Certainly, we are neither approving nor consenting to the acts of the Assembly. Indeed, we think that these circumstances require us to be publically silent for a time. When circumstances change, and we hope that, God willing, this happens soon, we will be able to speak in a more useful way.

To our beloved son, Dominic of Rochefoucault, Cardinal, Priest of the Holy Roman Church, Archbishop of Rouen
Pope Pius VI

To our beloved son: health and our apostolic blessing.

Every day we are afflicted with deeper sorrow on your account and on account of the events in your country that our messengers continue to inform us about. However, after reading your letter of the 9 January, our paternal heart was thrown into an even deeper grief because of what it contained. It is shocking to see the great many losses that the Church in France has suffered. We groan within and are almost overwhelmed by hearing of your most tragic humiliations. Not only do we share your sorrow, because these difficulties are not foreign to us, but we also feel that we share in the wounds that you have suffered.

What consolation can we offer you in the midst of such trials, as we try to imagine ourselves suffering in those same trials? We do not see ourselves as having recourse to any human means, but the effect of this should not be that we give ourselves over to despair. Instead, we put all of our hope in God. He grants peace and consolation, and unites our prayers with his own. It is more efficacious to act in this way in the face of so many calamities. It is certain that we cannot neglect prayer. We began praying from the moment that we first heard of the dangerous acts which the entire nation of France has been subjected to. We have asked that God turn things for the better, that he might replace our sorrow with joy, that He might make his glory more and more clear, and that He might make our faith stronger.

In the meantime, for you to see our zeal and good will towards you, we have freely assented to your request, given the difficult times that we are in, and to maintain ecclesiastical discipline as you desire, that the dispensation of religious vows should be entrusted solely to the prudence of the bishops. This is granted for individual cases through our ordinary apostolic power. We ask you in the Lord, that through these trials you might merit more grace in God's eyes for yourselves, for your churches, and for the entire nation of France. We lovingly and from the bottom of our heart give to you and your colleagues our apostolic blessing and a pledge of heavenly gifts.

Sent from Rome, the house of Saint Peter, under the ring of the fisherman, 31 March 1790, the sixteenth year of our Pontificate.

To our most dear brother in Jesus Christ, the very Christian Majesty, Louis XVI, King of France

Health and the apostolic blessing to our most beloved son in Christ.

We do not doubt, beloved son in Christ, to what a profound degree you adhere to the Catholic, Apostolic and Roman faith, the center of unity, to the Holy See, to our person, and to the faith of your fathers. Yet, we fear that your love for your subjects has been abused through deceitful cunning and subterfuge. They have perhaps abused your desire to rule over your kingdom with order and peace and to return it to its proper tranquility.

We represent Jesus Christ on earth. He has entrusted to Us the essentials of the faith. In a specific way the task falls on us, not only to help you remember your duties before God and your people (because we know that you would neither ever be unfaithful to your conscience, nor adopt the erroneous principles of vain political conduct), but from the fatherly love that our heart possesses for you, to make it well known to Your Majesty, and to clearly denounce, that if you sign into law the decrees relating to the clergy in France, you will lead your county into a host of errors. You will subject your regime to a schism, and you could make a cruel war against religion more probable. We have tried to take all necessary precautions to avoid being guilty of the charge of adding fuel to these flames. So far, we have only opposed them in a harmless way, with the weapons of prayer directed to God. But, if the attacks on religion continue, the head of the Church will speak publically. He will shout. But, of course, he will always do so motivated by a spirit of charity. Certainly we have duties to the world, but our first duty is to God.

Beware, dearly beloved son in Christ, do not think that that a political and civil assembly has the power to change the doctrine and the discipline of the Universal Church, or to oppose and count as nothing the teachings of the Fathers and Councils. They cannot summarily reorder the hierarchy of the Church. They cannot determine the way the Church chooses her Bishops. They cannot unilaterally suppress dioceses. In a phrase, they cannot justly throw the Church into disorder and deform her in such a way that she no longer looks like the Church.

Your Majesty has two archbishops in your realm. One of them has tirelessly defended the rights of religion against the attacks of unbelievers. The other possesses a deep knowledge of dogma and discipline. Consult them. Take advantage of the bishops and wise men in your country, those who are distinguished by their piety and their wisdom. For the good of your own eternal soul and the souls of your people, do not imprudently give your approval to a series of decrees that will offend the Catholics in your realm and cause them great scandal.

You have undone many things in the pursuit of the perceived good of your nation. It may very well be in your power to renounce the power that is yours by right. But even if you have this right, you lack the right to lessen or deny in anything that is owed to God and to the Church. Remember; you are her first-born son.

We have explained our concerns as the spiritual head of the Church. We have given these matters the highest priority. We have turned them over again and again in our mind. And, they have filled us with sorrow. But we have another cause for concern, which has also become troublesome. You know that Avignon has revolted from us. By doing so, it has fallen under the power of the revolutionaries in France. But we think that the revolutionaries are hardened in their position. They will never accept what we offered. And so, they will completely reject the loyalty that they owe you. The result of such an example (besides the obvious violation of your rights) is that you will never be able to reclaim your proper authority over the nation of France, especially when your provinces revolt from you, and they change their loyalty to another nation. There is no doubt that such a thing may come to pass throughout your entire realm as it is swept up in the revolutionary spirit.

But we have confidence in Divine Providence, and, with a steadfast commitment to the faith of our fathers, we trust that we will obtain the help that we have sought. With respect to that which concerns both of us, you can be assured that we will give this matter our utmost attention, to the point of anguish. We will only be at peace when we know you are at peace and flourishing.

It is with a deep paternal affection that we offer our apostolic benediction to Your Majesty and your august family.

To our venerable brother Jean-George, archbishop of Vienne
Pope Pius VI

To our venerable brother: health and apostolic blessings.

The most recent decrees from the National Assembly concerning ecclesiastical matters are full of errors to the point that they are not even laws. They are erroneous, because they are founded on false principles. They are not laws at all, because they do not come from the proper authority. We are writing to you so that you will know how deep is our concern and how intense is our sorrow.

But we also want to impress upon you how deep and inconsolable our sorrow will be if the most Christian King of France were to give his sanction to these decrees! If the royal authority were to act in this way, it would lead to a schism. As a result communication would be cut between the realm in France and the center of unity, which has been placed by divine institution in the Apostolic Chair that we hold. This King, who possesses such a glorious Christian name, will be called to account for a schism. What a sad event this would be! We should do what we can to prevent this from happening. If the realm were to adopt these laws, then every bishop elected under them would enter into schism. That would force us to declare them outside of the communion of the faithful. To see a vast empire lost during our pontificate, one that has contributed so much good to the Church, would deeply wound our heart. We would see the victory of the powers of disbelief. Their intentions are obvious: they are not only refusing to declare the Catholic religion the predominant one in the realm, but they will certainly also seek to destroy its name. As a consequence, they will lead countless victims into a terrible state.

As yet, we have kept silent. We do not want to irritate the fury of the revolutionaries any further. At the same time, we have not stopped asking for Divine Aid in our public and private prayers. Now, as we see them coming closer to even greater dangers, we are starting to think that it is no longer prudent to remain silent. And so, to begin our efforts, we wrote directly to the King. Today, we have sent out a letter written in a simple and friendly style to begin using all the means at our disposal, so that he does not approve the decrees, that he do nothing to give them the weight of his authority. I cannot go in person to speak to the King. This method, of course, would be the most efficacious. And so, I am asking you, my venerable brothers in the episcopate, you who live in that nation, to get through to him.

You are among the bishops of France, and you are the most capable person I know for carrying out such an important task. More than once, you have proven yourself to be a zealous witness to and defender of good doctrine. Since, then, there is little time to lose in carrying out this important task, based on the trust that we have in your capabilities, we hope that you take up this task carefully and with energy. In fulfilling it, you will protect your religion, your King, and your country from worse evils. It will no doubt be possible for you to speak heart to heart with the King. Do all you can to convince him to oppose these fatal decrees, even if his adversaries threaten his resistance with a host of dangers. He should remember that there is never a good reason to dissemble in matters relating to the truth, even if he has the intention of reversing his decision when circumstances improve.

If after reflecting on these matters you are able to take a clear position with the King, emphasizing the importance of the Gospels, we promise you that Our Lord Jesus Christ will grant you many graces. We very much hope that your honorable undertaking will be able to achieve the most beneficial results, which other good men strongly desire along with us. We ask Our Lord that he have mercy on your efforts, and we affectionately give you, as a measure of our benevolence, our apostolic blessing.

Given in Rome, at Saint Mary Major, 10 July 1790, the sixteenth year of our pontificate.

Signed, Pius.

To our venerable brother Jerome-Marie, Archbishop of Bordeaux
Pope Pius VI

Venerable brother, health and apostolic blessing to you.

The confidence that we have gained, because of the openness that you showed in your letter to us, has inspired our apostolic zeal. It has moved me to encourage you in your zeal. These times require an abundance of it, because the monarch in France is being led into a deep morass. You know this, being a witness to the most violent agitation. They have swept up and almost overwhelmed the city and the entire empire in only a few months. When we heard of these things, we judged it better to remain silent for a time. We hoped to not further provoke those responsible for this violence to even greater violent acts. During this time, we have had constant recourse to the grace of God through public and private prayers. We have asked him for peace and for a restoration of order in the realm of France. We now see that the disorders afflicting your country are only growing. The judges of that land have shown their incompetence by allowing the government to stretch out her hands and steal the property of the Church. And so, we can no longer keep silent. We must pay the debt that we owe to the Truth and let her break out in freedom.

The new decrees that the National Assembly have passed openly attack the unity of the Catholic Church; they will break all lines of communication between France and the Church. If the King gives them his approval, he will lead the French Church into a schism. We would like to avoid seeing the very Christian King of France become a schismatic. Bishops elected under the provision of the new law would become schismatic as well. It would then fall under our responsibility to declare them usurpers, and to do the same for any priest that placed himself under their jurisdiction. You can clearly see, venerable brother, that the revolutionaries have as their goal to reduce the Catholic religion to a mere name. These decrees will strengthen unbelievers in their resolve. They use freedom of speech as a pretext for advancing their agenda. But this freedom is fleeting and unstable. It can only lead to moral chaos.

We have the duty to vigorously oppose these criminal plans, God willing, with all of the reasonable means at our disposal. And so, we have judged it appropriate to call on the aid of our venerable brother bishops in France, in particular those who have access to the King. We have advised them to persuade this excellent prince to avoid giving his approval to these poisonous decrees. It is in this spirit that we have also made it a priority to address you before all others. Your reputation is such that we believe he has great trust in you. We probably do not have to remind you of the responsibilities that you accepted when you were ordained a bishop. No doubt, you firmly understand how serious this matter is. You have to prevent the King from approving these fatal decrees, not only for his own good, but also for the good of his people and the entire kingdom: that is, the Common Good.

We understand that he is in a very difficult situation. The revolutionaries have stirred up the masses, and they are ready for violent action. But we also know that, in this matter, he cannot fold in the face of the frantic multitude. If they are allowed to break away from their sacred chains, they will then only listen to the Furies, who will lead them like lemmings off the edge of a cliff. Men cannot change the lines that connect us to God. The King cannot dissemble in this matter for any reason. He cannot do so, thinking that he can hold a different intention in his heart during this terrible set of circumstances and then act upon that intention when the circumstances have improved.

We have sent by the same courier a letter to the King. We wrote this letter in a simple style, reminding him of his duties, and trying to spur him on to constancy and fortitude in fulfilling them. But you are able to bend his ear. You can be much more effective than I by speaking to him in person. We have complete confidence that with the help of heaven your efforts will be crowned with a happy success. We await your response in the hopes that will give some consolation to our heart, which, up until now, has been filled with sorrow. In addition, after beseeching the Holy Spirit to inspire you to say what is most opportune and most prudent, we send you our apostolic blessing from the bottom of our heart.

Sent from Rome, Saint Mary Major, 10 July 1790, the sixteenth year of our Pontificate.

Signed Pius.

To our venerable brother Jean-François, Bishop of Saint-Pol-de-Léon
Pope Pius VI

Venerable brother: we wish you health and we give you our apostolic blessing.

Evils shake the Church in France, and you see them getting worse each day. On June 28, you wrote us a letter describing them, and we have received it. We are fully aware of the outrageous efforts of the revolutionaries to wipe out the Church that made France a beacon to the world. Of course, these reports fill our heart with sorrow. It seem that this epoch is filled with disasters – disasters that, like a flood, are threatening to drown us. We are almost overwhelmed. We cannot imagine enduring anything as bitter and as deeply distressing as these events. Any course of action at this point is full of danger. For quite some time we have been asking the Father of lights for his aid. We have also asked for public and private prayers, so that he might lead and protect us in our weakness, for the good of the Church. We are attending to difficult matters, and always need to remember to beg the assistance of Divine Mercy. We have done what is possible to form the piety and faith of the very Christian King. We hope to prevent him from remaining silent. In addition, we forbade him from giving his consent to the scandalous decrees that the National Assembly has produced. They can only lead to schism and the further advance of erroneous ideas. We have also had recourse to those among our brothers in the episcopate who have the possibility of seeing the King and speaking frankly with him. We wrote to them to encourage them in the Lord, and we asked them, with all the influence that our ministry carries, to come to the aid of the Church, religion, and the nation of the prince himself, for whom the title 'very Christian' is as dear as it is glorious. May God grant his Mercy on our efforts, that he might hear our vows to work for the good, and that he might confound and ruin by his Divine Power the plots of wicked men.

We admire your integrity, especially when it comes to Catholic Doctrine. You also have shown true priestly fortitude in the way that you have opposed the novel decrees of the National Assembly, which lack any legitimate authority. You are correct in thinking that no person or political body has the right to exercise authority over a bishop or to change the structure of dioceses without the approval of the Holy See. With respect to the question of what you should do when violence has snatched your flock from you, it is difficult to determine what charity requires. The responsibilities of a pastor can change often according to times and circumstances. You may recall that our predecessors took different approaches to handling themselves during times of persecution. Some exposed themselves to danger. Others, without any known duplicity, withdrew themselves from events. This is why Christ Our Lord advised his apostles to be as innocent as doves and as cunning as serpents. He did not want them to agonize over what they would say or do before the powers of this world. But such is the thought of this age, and the revolutionary spirit grows so strong in France, that we are not certain how to animate the zeal of the bishops in France without exposing them to further danger. Such is the response that we believe we ought to give to your letter. We assure you of our support and profound admiration. We affectionately give you and the flock entrusted to your care, from the bottom of our heart, our apostolic blessing, as a witness to our pontifical benevolence.

Given in Rome, from Saint Mary Major, 4 August 1790, the sixteenth year of our pontificate.

Callistus Marininus, secretary of His Holiness for letters written in latin.

To our dearly beloved son in Jesus Christ, his very Christian Majesty, Louis, King of France
Pope Pius VI

May God grant health and our apostolic blessing to our very dear son in Jesus Christ.

The letter that Cardinal de Bernis has sent us on behalf of You Majesty, our dearly beloved son in Christ, shows the respect that you have for religion as well as the love you have for the Holy See. You had good reason to believe that you should consult us so that you might not err when it came to matters that touch on the universal discipline of the Church and canon law. The oldest son of the Church knows that the spiritual authorities and the temporal authorities ought to give each other mutual aid. In this context, some rights belong to the Church alone, to the exclusion of the power of a political assembly, to make laws about spiritual things. The temporal authorities can do little more in these matters other than observe. The most they can do is offer assistance in carrying them out. If we fail to keep the proper relationship between the spiritual and the temporal authorities, then all law and order will be overturned. Confusion will reign in the public square. Schism will take the place of the happy harmony that ties together all the faithful of the Church into one community.

Whenever the Church is tossed about by waves in a storm, for some of that time she must oppose her enemies with patience. But this does not mean that she loosens in any manner her firm commitment to live everything that the Catholic faith requires. It is with this principle in mind that we have for several years dealt with matters in France. We neither thought it necessary to speak publically, nor to rush out in righteous anger when a spirit of opinion and error swept up the country, fostering madness. We prepared ourselves in this manner, so that when the emotions calmed down we could help everybody see the basic principles of belief and the norms of the Gospels.

Perhaps several bishops in your country have wondered why we remained silent. They have been waiting for our voice to be heard with force and solemnity. Your Majesty can assure them that we have been doing much to defend religion against such attacks, which for quite some time have been coming from your country in writings filled with the poison of disbelief. We have not yet shouted from the rooftops. But we have also not yet dissimulated the truth. We hope that you will act according to such high principles. We hope that fear does not lead you to put the ministers of the altar in danger. We cannot do anything that might harm the religion of which we are in different degrees instruments.

Be strong, beloved son in Christ, so that you can in turn strengthen other souls. Encourage them to be patient in the face of difficulties. And to work for the true stability that comes from living by and implementing true principles, what the Catholic Church prescribes. You can be sure that the violence that has broken out against your authority is a scourge that God has sent. It is his way of correcting a revolutionary people so that they might once again respect the right order of law. Wise bishops will stand out because they act this way: they will unceasingly ask God to help them. We are doing the same; that is, we ask God the Redeemer that he might shorten this time of trial and show us mercy. At the same time, can anyone be surprised when God is irritated due to the crimes of men? We can certainly hope that the current evils that we face will be lessened. The first goal of their ministry should be to exercise their spiritual duties, to make sure that no one steals their churches. But what has just been done, namely, this theft of churches, is a loss that will affect them more than anything else. This is a superior good upon which all their other responsibilities depend.

Given the importance of the situation, we have decided to gather together a group of Cardinals. We are going to take up and study the articles of the decrees, as you have asked us to do through Cardinal de Bernis. There is a possibility that we might not be able to get a messenger through to you in order to communicate to you the content of our deliberations. The Cardinal, the minister of Your Majesty, has asked us to respond quickly to your letters, before the Cardinals meet. So, we have decided today to write our first thoughts to you, but later, we will send you a more detailed response. We grant our apostolic blessing, from the bottom of our heart, to you and to your august family.

Rome, Saint Mary Major, 17 August 1790, the sixteenth year of our pontificate.

To our venerable brother Toussaint-François-Joseph, bishop of Quimper
Pope Pius VI,

Venerable brother: may God grant you health and our apostolic blessing.

We are worried to the point of sickness about what is happening in France, and your fraternal letter of 11 July only sharpens the pain that we feel in our heart. The deepest sorrow comes from hearing how much the powers of license have harmed the Catholic religion. They have placed it in a most precarious position. We know that God sees everything. He knows the fervor that exists in our hearts. We will not do anything to run away from the responsibilities that are part of our apostolic position. We are mindful of the integrity of religion, the dignity of the episcopate, and that Catholics in France might exercise their faith in tranquility. But we are not able to stand by and remain indifferent when the revolutionaries undertake plans to overturn everything. We have sought the advice of a congregation of Cardinals, as is custom, in order to understand better what are these new things that are attacking the foundations of the Church in France. We are waiting for a response from our brothers in the episcopate in France. This will help us in our own deliberations. Then we will be able to give a response to the very Christian King of France who has consulted us about what he should do so as to achieve the common good in his country. For all these reasons, venerable brother, you can see why at this moment we cannot grant you the powers that you are asking for. At the same time, we are impressed by the fortitude and the piety that you openly showed in your distinguished writings. You have also shown great strength in defending your diocese in the face of actions coming from an illegitimate authority and under the threat of real violence. May the Lord, in his ineffable Mercy, increase every day the strength of the pastors of the Church in proportion to the dangers that threaten them. Accept, then, our apostolic blessing, which comes from the tender affection of our heart and which we offer to you, venerable brother, and to your flock.

Given in Rome, Saint Mary Major, 1 September 1790, the sixteenth year of our pontificate.

Callistus Marinius, secretary of His Holiness for Latin letters.

To our dear son in Jesus Christ, the very Christian Majesty, Louis XVI the King of France
Pope Pius VI

To our very dear son in Jesus Christ: health and our apostolic blessing.

Our heart is troubled to learn that you have given your approval to the unjust decrees of the National Assembly. We know that you felt forced to do this, because you find yourself in circumstances in which violence and tyranny are emanating from the same Assembly. The Assembly had previously given its sanction without consulting us, especially on the question of how to respect the rights of consciences, in order to avoid creating the scandal of dissent among the Catholics living there, and to prevent the almost irreparable damage that is caused by a schism.

We have noticed that since you have taken the throne you have in truth shown yourself to have strong religious sentiments, concern for the Holy See, and filial affection towards us. And so it causes us even greater sorrow to see you, a great King, coerced by the violence of the National Assembly to approve their decrees that are directed against the foundations of the Catholic religion.

If you had been educated in all the principles of the disciplinary organization of the Church, then a teacher would have exposed you to all the decrees of canon law, the age-old sense of the Gallican Church, the tradition of the Church going back to the Fathers of the Church. He would also have explained how some aspects of the disciplinary organization of the Church come so close as to touch on dogma itself as well as the essence and nature of religion. Then you would see, with the help of all the certitude that evidence brings, that these novel decrees have as their goal nothing more than to use your name as a shield for their criminal actions. You would also see what few dare to say openly: that these acts are simply the result of the disbelief and hard-headedness that are at the foundation of the thought of this century. And now we urge you, beloved son in Christ, to look into your heart and see God, your Creator and your Judge. He has wished to preserve the faith of your fathers for many long centuries and through many political storms. He will also work wonders for you, if like your fathers did, you remain strong in holding yourself to his laws. He will also kindle the fire of love that the people of France held of old for the King. He has always been the single reason that France has achieved glory. He will also restore peace to the kingdom of France because he is the source of all political power.

Your Majesty seems surprised, as though you had not received my letter in response to the letter that you sent through Cardinal de Bernis. In that letter, I responded to the most important questions that you asked me through the Cardinal. But we assure you that we have not delayed one minute in attending to the difficult task that you have asked us to study. Without any delay, we have called twenty Cardinals trained as theologians and canon lawyers to a council. We have begun our task of studying the circumstances. Of course, it did take some time to gather together the necessary documents and copy them. We are also waiting for some information that only Cardinal de Bernis, your envoy to the Vatican, can give us. It is impossible at this time for us to obtain this information from any other source. His Eminence did not put off any effort in attempting to obtain from us an answer to your pressing questions, but, at the same time, he also saw that we could not let anything interrupt our work at this point. There are many considerations to account for in order to properly act in these circumstances. One cannot easily know what to do at first glance.

So that the successor of Saint Peter can arrive at definitive doctrinal statement after a mature examination, he should have some assurance that those who seek his counsel will be docile when they hear his voice. But who is there to help bring about this docility in a time of disorder, of madness and of unrestrained passions? Can anyone truly say whether our manner of acting will bring about good or evil? To be sure, given the passions which currently rule in France, we are more fearful of the evil effects than we are hopeful of the good ones.

All calculation can be done away with, and all hope is lost, if the center of unity in the Church loses his moral authority as well as his influence on souls. We hope that the several observations that we have just made, as well as other ones, which are also important, will convince you how necessary it is in this instance to proceed only after a serious and mature examination of principles and events. The consistory of Cardinals will begin here in Rome on the 24th of this month. Each one will give his opinion in writing. Then, we will weigh how each would influence religion, prudence, peace and concord. We will also ask God to help us and to enlighten us with the rays of his Divine Light.

Up until this moment, we have delayed giving our just condemnation against the decrees of the civil constitution of the clergy. Our affection for you and the soft place that we have in our heart for your rule have led us to take a middle way. No one should forget that we hold the position of the common father of the faithful, that your subjects are my spiritual children, and that you are the oldest son of the Church. Our first obligation is to carry out our responsibilities in a spirit of paternal charity. We do not want to use spiritual punishments too quickly against our sons who are deceived and placed in difficult circumstances because of the break out of a reckless passion. You are not revolutionaries or hard-headed resistors of legitimate authority. We have fought the violence of revolution with patience. We have opposed fluctuations and inconstancy of passion with leniency and detachment. We have entrusted ourselves to Divine Help and asked that, without us having to say something striking in public, He might restore religion to its rightful place, allow each one to live a happy life, restore political order, and bind together in social harmony. We ask also that those who have committed the crime of neglecting or even outraging religion might renounce their difficulties and allow it to once again enter into their hearts. We wait for the day when the commitments that we have made come to the best possible conclusion.

We have also asked the bishops of your country to have recourse to us with complete confidence. We want to respond to their concerns. We want to help them in their efforts to put correct principles into effect. We want to work with them so that we do not do anything that compromises true peace. We hope to avoid any actions or insults that could lead to schism or any of its effects. For your part, our beloved son in Christ, we urge you to work with us to heal with the appropriate medicine any evils that have occurred. We should search for ways to give space to erring souls so that they can return to the path. We should draw people to right reason. We can also inspire them by our exemplary life of virtue, charity, constancy and fortitude. With this way of acting, we will be able to more easily repair the damage that has been done and to rebuild in the future on the foundation of right reason. They are entering into counsel with us. They should not be apprehensive. They should have recourse to us, given the distressing circumstances in which they find themselves.

This is the plan that we hope to follow. We are not going to use any of our provisional powers. These often do not satisfy anyone. Instead, they often lead to more difficulties and the subversion of the discipline, hierarchy, and jurisdiction of the Church. We are very far from despairing that God will convert hearts and enlighten spirits.

If, after deliberating with the greater part of the apostolic college, God further inspires us to a more efficacious plan, one that is rooted in wisdom, we will communicate it to Your Majesty as soon as possible. In the meanwhile, we affectionately extend to you and to your august family our paternal and apostolic blessing.

Given in Rome at Saint Mary Major, 22 September 1790, the sixteenth year of our pontificate.

To our Venerable brother, Louis-Charles, Bishop of Amiens,
Pope Pius VI

Venerable brother: may God grant you health and our apostolic blessing.

Many calamities have become part of the apostolic ministry that Divine Providence has entrusted to me. But we have just learned about the saddest of all. It is part of the consequences of the revolution that has risen in France. Seeing the evils that afflict the entire nation has inspired us to respond. First, we continually pray in public and private to the Father of Mercy. Second, we have constantly sought the counsel of wise men. And we do not want to hide from you, venerable brother in Christ, that we have gathered together a consistory of Cardinals in order to formulate an answer to the questions that the very Christian King of France has asked of us. The consistory has formulated the measures that it thinks are the best ones to take in these circumstances. We understand that the circumstances are dangerous and complicated. We understand that they require detached study to get to the heart of the matter. We cannot go beyond the limits that have been set by our ancestors. So far, we do not have a definitive answer from the consistory. But, we can say the following to your questions and to those that the King has posed to us. We have granted to all the bishops of France the indult for dispensing with the canonical impediments to marriage. To your letter of 13 August in which you ask certain questions, we have added this response to the general one that we have already given. We are moved by the highest motives of charity and affection towards you for the zeal that you show in remaining in your diocese and for remaining loyal to us. We are happy to grant to you, in the one case that you have presented to us, the faculty to dispense from our authority for the impediment of the second line of consanguinity in a collateral line for a man from your diocese. According to the circumstances described in your letter, there is no time for delay. As for you, my venerable brother, as a witness to the fraternal affection we share, we impart on you permanently our apostolic blessing.

Given at Rome, Saint Mary Major, 26 September 1790, the sixteenth year of our pontificate.

Callistus Marinius, secretary of the Holy Father for Latin letters.

Letter of Pope Pius VI to the Bishop of Basle
Pope Pius VI

Venerable Brother: may God grant you salvation. We give your our apostolic blessing.

Nothing causes us more concern in these times, venerable brother, than the decrees that the National Assembly in France has forced on us, the bishops of France, and their dioceses. We know that this has also caused you great worry, as we have seen from your letter of 11 November 1790. You rightly fear a revolution against holy things, and you see that it is spreading to your diocese in Alsace and that it presents many difficulties to the souls entrusted to your care. You have rightly consulted us and presented to us several doubts that you have about how to best proceed. To begin, we would like to make it clear to you that, at this moment, nothing has come to us relating to the election of a new bishop for upper Alsace. In second place, even if such a request were made to us, it would be difficult to grant our approval, given the present circumstances.

If a bishop were presented under this new illegitimate form, we would consider him installed without our consent and without the consent of the Holy See. We would consider him an intruder. You can easily understand this; you would not summarily hand over to another bishop the authority that you currently exercise in Alsace. That is the area of your jurisdiction. A new bishop is not able to licitly and validly exercise power there. Our consent is required in order to establish a new bishop or a new diocese. We want to assure you in writing in a way that you can be sure that no one could ever dare to claim otherwise, that the way things are established now for electing bishops will always remain so. This should provide the key to the answers that you need for all of your questions. We want you know with certainty that we have no intention of changing the borders of dioceses. We do not want to disturb the rights of the ancient churches unless there is a serious reason to do so and the circumstances themselves were to lead the local bishops to wish to do so. In the meantime, we all should agree to the same thing, that we should offer constant prayers to almighty God sothat he might grant his mercy and his all-powerful protection to his Church which is currently being tossed about in such a violent storm. We should also ask that he send those who have been entrusted with the government of the Church a spirit of fortitude and that he might help them persevere in it. We permanently grant you, venerable brother, our apostolic blessing.

Given at Rome, the house of Saint Peter under the ring of the fisherman, 11 December 1790, the sixteenth year of our pontificate.

Brief addressed to M. l'abbé Thoumin Desvauspons, vicar general of the Diocese of Dol
Pope Pius VI

Our dear son: may God grant you salvation and our apostolic blessing.

Your letter of 26 December has shown us wonderful evidence of genuine piety and love for the discipline of the Church. It has also filled us with great consolation. But we have been most of all spiritually affected by the zeal that inspires your actions. It is a fine compliment to your deep knowledge of doctrine, and it is of great credit to you.

We have studied all the parts of your letter, our dear son, and we are well aware of all of your circumstances, even down to the smallest detail. And having looked over everything, we can do nothing but praise the action that you have taken in this matter. It is good that, not only did you not accept your nomination, but that you decisively rejected it. You rightly saw that it violates all accepted canonical forms that have been practiced with rigor for so long in the Church. Your stance of dissent, the lines that you have drawn and the position that you have staked out and made public, has proven that you take as holy and respect the rules of the Church. You have shown that you will be able to handle difficult situations in the future that might test your piety or your fortitude.

We have also tried to understand what motivates your bishop. We love him with fraternal charity, and it is a heavy burden for us to have to make a judgment about him, but we have considered the matter before God, and we do not think that you should, in any way, deviate from your initial refusal. It is preferable in a case such as this one to remain constant in your refusal. It is easy to see that any relaxation of discipline is dangerous in a time when license and perversity have infected the highest circles of society. We ought to hope also that your refusal becomes public knowledge. Due to your good reputation, your good example will encourage those who wish to uphold the holy laws of the Church to persevere in the good by the Mercy of God. It will confirm them in their good resolutions. And those who unfortunately have abandoned their duties might be strengthened by your example and inspired to return to the right path.

Dear son, we have sought to provide an answer to your letter without delay. We have a firm hope that you will continue in your good resolutions. For just cause we can rejoice in your good example and we hold you in greater and greater esteem. We look forward to the day that we can see you in this city. We wholeheartedly commend you for all of your work and study to defend true religion. While you strive to accomplish what you have indicated in your letter, God will show us, as well as your bishop, what task he wishes to give you in his vineyard. We end giving you our apostolic blessing with all of the affection of our heart.

Given at Rome, 2 February 1791, the sixteenth year of our pontificate.

Callistus, secretary of His Holiness for Latin letters.

To our Venerable brother Elléon, bishop of Toulon
Pope Pius VI

Venerable brother in Jesus Christ: may God grant you salvation and our apostolic blessing.

Your letter of 17 January brought us tears of sorrow and filled us with confusion. Along with you, we are urgently beseeching God day and night on account of the persecution which the wicked of the world have raised against the Church in these bitter days. We spare no work so that we might carry out our responsibilities. We remain hopeful that God will always fulfill the good that he has promised for his Church, and that she will never collapse under the weight of persecution. In the meantime, what sustains our weakness and grants our soul consolation is to see the fortitude of the French bishops. The vigor with which they are upholding the holy discipline of the Church and the heroic zeal with which they are defending canon law have made them an example before angels and men. We have not ceased to ask God to grant us examples of constancy and fortitude. Above all, we hope that there will be examples of charity towards all. These will add to the beauty of the Church and conquer the hard-heartedness of her enemies. We have known for quite some time that you deserve a place high on the list of defenders of the Faith. Your recent letter only further confirms this. You have written to your flock with all the zeal that you are capable of mustering. You have urged them and encouraged them to be faithful to their duties as Christians. You have done it in writing, because prudence has led you to see that you cannot speak to them in person. Do not be disheartened by the number of clergy who have decided to follow under the banners of this age. With such a great revolution striking the republic, it would be best to see their prevarication as that of a fearful heart falling into a trap by seduction. It is not a case of hard-heartedness. We can hope for a quick return to the fold, especially because you know how to prudently weave together firmness with gentleness when carrying out your pastoral task. A sign of your good sense and what should make stronger the hope that inspires you is that a number of bishops from other dioceses in France have already repented of their false steps. May the God of Mercy strengthen you in virtue so that you may better endure these calamitous days. As a sign of the affection that we hold in our heart for you, venerable brother, we give you, from the bottom of our heart, our apostolic blessing.

Given at Rome, Saint Peter, 9 February 1791, the sixteenth year of our pontificate.

Callistus Marinius, secretary of His Holiness for Latin letters.

To our dear son Etienne-Charles de Loménie de Brienne, Cardinal-priest of the Holy Roman Church, Archbishop of Sens
Pope Pius VI

Health and apostolic blessing to our venerable son.

Even before I received your first letter, my dear son, I have been preoccupied studying the opinions of the bishops in France who have taken the Oath of Loyalty as dictated by the decrees of the National Assembly. There are about thirty in the group and they have consulted the Holy See. You have also written. You have all asked for instructions about how to oppose such an undertaking from the civil authority. It cannot escape your notice that these decrees, thus far practically unheard of among Catholics, alienate and return to a servile status that Catholic religion, which has always been predominant in this realm. The same acts steal the goods of the Church, deprive her of her ministers, and deny her rights. These ought to be respected as holy and inviolate.

We had barely read your letter, before we immediately understood that your way of thinking seems to deviate from the pure and right opinions of your colleagues, which are also our opinions. Indeed, a certain rumor has increased our suspicion of this. It has brought home to us that you adhere too much to the opinions of the innovators, and that you might even favor their designs. We have delayed writing to you for two reasons. First, we have been tirelessly preparing our response to the bishops of France, which will also apply to you. Second, we do not wish to expose your reasons for acting, and to attribute some fault to you, without first having certain proof and not relying only on rumors.

We have almost completed our response to the bishops of France, and this letter should also answer a number of your questions. However, while we were writing this letter, we heard of new deeds of yours. Then, against my expectations, I received a second letter from you, dated 30 January. In that letter, you show a certain indifference towards the opinion of the majority of the bishops of France. They justify their actions under the pretext of the tyranny of necessity. You have indicated to us that you have resolved to create a new clergy in your Cathedral church. Necessity has required this of you because you have taken over the government of part of another diocese. And, you have also taken the Oath as required by the National Assembly. You have sent us the formula of the Oath and you have indicated to us that you have neither given your interior consent to it nor to all the actions of the Assembly. Their authority is limited to certain areas of discipline in your diocese, and in this aspect its authority comes through you. The decrees of the National Assembly require your authority, and by your authority you can bring out their illegitimate parts and purge them.

To all of these things you have added, that thus far you have not installed the priest of Gommecourt, elected as the new priest of Versailles. But, you fear that this priest will keep repeating his requests. Others will demand the same thing. At some point, you will be reduced to granting what they demand or you will be forced to abandon your own office. By expressing yourself in this way, you seem to indicate that you actually prefer the former, especially by the way you express yourself: I fear that this extreme measure might come to pass, that I could be forced to compromise something that touches on my sacred purple, because I can foresee the evils that would result for my diocese.

We cannot explain in words how much it pains us to see you write such opinions publically. They are unbecoming of a great man – a man given the dignity of an Archbishop and shining with the honor of a Cardinal. But now is not the time and this is not the place to show you the errors into which you have fallen. We will note, in passing, that you are not able to bring greater dishonor to the purple color than in taking the Oath of Loyalty and in carrying out its decrees, and destroying the ancient center of your church. You usurped the territory of another diocese put into your hands by the civil power. These are detestable deeds.

Read Canon Four of the Council of Lyon, and you will see it expressly stated that, when necessity makes the bishop absent, no one should dare to take his place, to offer the Eucharist in his place, or to celebrate the mystery of ordination. If someone has the audacity to rush to take such actions, he is not only reproved by the Council, but he has already deprived himself of unity with his brothers. What you have done is abhorrent to common sense. You have acted in a way that is illegitimate, thinking that by this gesture you could purify the force of the decrees of the National Assembly. Finally, you have bound yourself to an oath that contradicts holier and more solemn sacraments that you have received. You ought not to have forgotten that you are also bound by them. But now you have promised to carry out what is contained in the Civil Constitution of the Clergy, and that is no more than a collection of a number of heresies.

You erroneously and shamelessly rationalize your fault by claiming that your oath-taking was simply an exterior act, separating it from the interior act of the spirit. A certain philosopher commented on this: he imagined such a way of acting and found it completely shameful for an honest man, who would abhor what is proposed: embracing something as if he were someone else when committing to the content the Oath. Whenever a doctrine such as this has appeared, the Church has not failed to condemn it and prohibit men from acting this way. A response will be sent to the bishops of France and will make plain the depravity of your errors. The letter will also indicate the penalties required by canon law. It will be with great sadness in our heart that we will have to apply these penalties to you. You will be deprived of your dignity as a Cardinal unless you retract in a satisfactory way the public scandal that you have caused.

In the meantime, our paternal heart moves us, to spare you from committing new faults, and to interpret a time of silence as consent to your errors. So, we wrote to you without delay, to urge you in the Lord, not to take any new steps. Above all, please do not have the audacity to ordain new bishops who would be schismatics, thinking that this would not harm the Church. According to the decrees of the Council of Trent, this power rests solely in the Apostolic See. If a priest or a metropolitan takes this power upon himself, our apostolic office requires us to declare schismatic both those who do the ordinations and those who are ordained. All of their future acts would be declared null and void. We have already explained this in a letter to our dear son in Jesus Christ, Louis XVI, the King of France, as well as to the Archbishops of Bordeaux and Vienne, on the 8 and 9 of July 1790. We will explain the same thing in our response to all the bishops of France, which will appear shortly.

You are able to refuse ordaining a new bishop without punishment. Many of your colleagues have already refused to do it. In particular, the bishop of Rennes has not only refused to ordain a new bishop in

Quimper, but he has also shown in a learned and weighty discourse, how the decrees are contrary to ancient custom and violate the terms of the concordat. Almost all the bishops of France have shown great courage in refusing to take the Oath of Loyalty. They have identified those parts of the new constitution that touch on the authority of the Church. It should be clear now, that this necessity, which now seems to you so imminent, really does not exist. No one can free himself from the duties which tie him to God and to the Church. The threat of violence ought to increase the constancy and courage of true Christians. You should be ready to give public witness and even be willing to be subjected to exile or whatever other troubles could be stirred up by the imagination of this age.

The National Constitution promises Man freedom, by supposedly offering Man the right to think and write what occurs to him in religious matters. In reality, it fights against religion. It introduces novelties. It overturns the foundation of the authority of the Church. It denies her all of her rights. Your responsibility is to resist these errors. Follow the example of your colleagues. When the truth is not defended, it is oppressed. And then, a society gives free reign to vice. It fails to cut out evil and correct itself. Saint Felix III teaches that failing to beat down the perverse, doing nothing, is in fact to spur them on. In like manner, if someone suspects the existence of a secret society and does nothing to oppose their crimes, that person encourages the crime.

The current circumstances have nothing to do with the passage from Augustine that you refer to. Instead, it applies to a century in which the bishops and the popes were ready to suffer anything and to stand up to the greatest of evils rather than give up their rights or abandon the cause of God and of the Church. At the same time, many of your colleagues have by word and deed given a shining example in defense of religion. They have given an eloquent witness for all to see, something that is worth passing into eternal memory.

We hope that you will be docile to our advice and recognize your errors. In addition, we hope that you will distance yourself as far as possible from these novelties, that you will enter again into fulfilling your duties (which until now you have forgotten), that you will rejoin yourself to the other bishops who are one in doctrine, and that you will remain attached to the Holy See, in which resides the Magisterium, the Truth, and the center of unity. This is the way to avoid schism or any other error, or to correct it if it happens. This is what we see as possible, if the King, the most Christian prince, if the priests, if the entire nation hears the universal voice of the Truth, which is entrusted to us as the common father of all, and if the bishops remain united to their head and defend their bonds to him, and if they defend him with all of their energy. We will therefore not cease asking for Divine Help so that all the French might leave behind their errors that have preyed on their weakness and ignorance and that all of the plots of their enemies be foiled and cast into confusion. Indeed, these pretend to reform religion, but they are doing nothing other than subverting the foundations of the Catholic religion and the faith of our fathers.

In what remains, we would like to ask you and urge you again to return to the right path, to remain attached to the discipline of the Catholic Church, to show the chest of a bishop, and to distance yourself from all novelties, schisms, and errors. In these dangerous times, in these times of crisis, may you completely abandon yourself to Divine Counsel, to fortitude, to faith, and to spiritual patience. In order to further inspire you, we give our apostolic blessing to you, dear son, as well as to the flock entrusted to your care.

Given at Rome, 23 February 1791, the sixteenth year of our pontificate.

Brief to Cardinal de la Rochefoucault, Archbishop of Aix, and to the other Archbishops and Bishops of the National Assembly in France, on the Civil Constitution of the Clergy recently created by the French National Assembly
Pope Pius VI

To my dear sons and to my venerable brothers: may God grant you health and our apostolic blessing.

We are now responding to your letter of 10 October 1790. A great number of your venerable and illustrious colleagues had signed it. We have delayed our response a little due to the seriousness of the matter and because of an excessive number of urgent matters that we had to attend to. All of these matters have pierced our heart with deep, inconsolable sorrow. We first felt this sorrow when we learned that the National Assembly had convened to regulate matters concerning public economy, but then took their decrees to the point of attacking the Catholic Church. A majority of the conspirators have even gone one step further: they have forced their way into the sanctuary of the Church itself.

From the beginning, we have deemed it better to keep silent before this inconsiderate class of men, thinking that hearing the voice of Truth might further anger them and lead them to commit even worse evils than the ones they have already committed. We decided this following the authority of Saint Gregory the Great, who said: "Be discerning, and carefully consider the circumstances of tumultuous times. You ought to hold your tongue and not say things that make the situation more difficult." We first turned our prayers to God. We ordered public prayers to be said, so that his Spirit might penetrate the souls of these new lawmakers, and so that they might resolve to distance themselves from the philosophical principles of this age and instead attach themselves to the sound principles that our religion teaches. In this case, we have followed the example of Susanna, who, as Saint Ambrose explains, said more by her silence than if she had spoken. She remained silent before men but instead spoke to God. Her conscience spoke when her voice could not be heard. She did not seek the judgment of men, because she had God as her witness.

Furthermore, we have gathered together a consistory of our venerable brother Cardinals of the Holy and Roman Catholic Church. We began our meetings 23 March 1790. They have learned what has been done against the Catholic religion in France. We have shared with them the pain that we feel in our hearts. They have united their tears with ours, their prayers with ours.

While we were considering these matters, unexpected reports came to us in the middle of July. The National Assembly of France (by this name we usually understand the predominant number among them) passed a law under the pretext of the Civil Constitution of the Clergy. This law, to speak frankly, subverted the most sacred dogmas. It threw into confusion the time-tested ecclesiastical discipline. It destroyed the rights of the Holy See, the bishops, priests, as well as men's and women's religious orders. It undermined the rights of the entire Catholic community. It suppressed the most holy religious ceremonies. It deprived the Church of her ecclesiastical goods and benefits. It introduced other hardships so grave that one is hardly able to believe them unless one has suffered through them. We have been filled with dread since reading these decrees and the events surrounding them. They have produced in us the same impression that we see in one of our most illustrious predecessor, Gregory the Great, when he saw a certain letter that a bishop of Constantinople sent him to review. The first pages shocked him. They gave witness to the manifest depravity that was contained in the work. When all of the abovementioned sorrows had gathered in our heart, at the end of August our most beloved son in Christ, Louis, the very Christian King of France, sent us another letter. He asked us to take a position on, and perhaps even, at least provisionally, to approve with the weight of our authority, five articles of the civil constitution. He had already given them his royal sanction. To us the decrees seemed to violate canon law. Yet, we thought that we should be gentle with the King. We responded that we were going to hold a consistory of twenty Cardinals to examine the matter. We would put down all opinions in writing, so that we could weigh the matter in a way that corresponded to its seriousness. In another more familiar letter, we urged the King to consult the bishops in his kingdom. We trusted that they would give him good counsel and their frank opinions. It seemed obvious to us that together they could accomplish this task. Distance prevented us from advising the King in a more discrete manner, and we had to rely on this method in order to avoid causing any stain on our conscience. We have not received any explanation of your handling of these affairs. We have received published pastoral letters, sermons, and counsels full of evangelical spirit. Many bishops have produced such things. But these writings are published individually by their authors and not as a part of any plan. They did not indicate the things that you think you must do. And yet the critical moment required you to do this.

Then, we received your manuscript critiquing the principles of the civil constitution of the clergy. The manuscript begins with an extract of several decrees of the National Assembly. It then proceeds to offer many considerations that show the invalidity and the impropriety of the decrees. Almost at the same time, the King sent us yet another letter. He asked us to approve, at least provisionally, seven other decrees of the National Assembly. They were almost the same as the five decrees that he had sent us in August. One decree in particular caused us great sorrow. He gave his sanction to the decree of 27 November, which commanded that every bishop, vicar, parish priest, prefect of seminaries, and any other ecclesiastical functionary take an Oath of Loyalty to the constitutions within a certain period of time. Anyone failing to do this would be severely punished. We have repeated and confirmed what we had already declared and we will declare it again: that we will not make public our judgment of these decrees until we have heard what the majority of the bishops of France think of these matters.

The King has asked us, among other things, to convince the metropolitans and bishops to agree to the division and suppression of their archdioceses and dioceses. He has asked us to provisionally agree to retaining the canonical forms that the Church currently uses to erect new dioceses and to grant them the authority that is currently exercised by bishops and archbishops. Then, the new bishops will be able to install new parish priests according to the new mode of election, provided that no moral or doctrinal obstacle stands in the way of taking the position. One can see by this request of the King that he knows what good sense requires him to do in the case of bishops. And so, we should not make a judgment before hearing what they have to say. We waited, therefore, for your counsel as well as your reasons for your position, expressed in one voice from all of you or from as many of you as could be hoped for given the circumstances. This way of acting will put our ideas on a solid foundation. It will be the guide and standard of our deliberations. It will help us to make a judgment that is good for you and for the entire nation of France. While we have this expectation of you, we also can examine the letters that you have already sent us that contain all the articles of the Civil Constitution of the Clergy.

To begin, by reading the acts of the Council of Sens, assembled in 1527 to deal with the Lutheran heresies, we can better understand the principle and foundation that the national decrees follow. It cannot be exempt from the note of heresy, as the Council explains: "And after these ignorant men, Marsilius of Padua rose up. He wrote a poisonous book titled *Defensor Pacis*. The Lutherans have used it to shake up and bring great danger to Christian people. He treats the Church as an enemy and flatters the impiety of worldly princes. He contends that the bishop or prelate can only exercise exterior authority over those matters that the secular ruler has granted them power over. He argues that every priest exercises the same authority by virtue of the equality that Christ granted when He instituted the priesthood. This means that every priest, whether simple priests, bishops, archbishops, or even the Pope, have the same authority. If any priest has more power than another priest, it is only because a prince has freely granted this concession. The prince can revoke this power whenever he wishes to do so. Sacred Scripture refutes the monstrous madness of this deranged heretic. It clearly shows that ecclesiastical power does not derive from the power of the prince. It is founded on Divine Right. The Church has its own authority to pass laws for the good of its faithful. It has the right to impose penalties on those who rebel against it from within. The Scriptures also show the ecclesial power to be a very different power than the lay power. It is not only a higher power, but is a power that carries with it greater dignity. Despite these arguments, this Marsilius and other heretics rage with impiety against the Church, doing whatever they can to diminish her legitimate authority."

Again, you may remember the judgment of Benedict XIV of happy memory. His judgment agreed with that of the Council. He wrote to the primate, archbishops, and bishops of Poland on 5 March 1752 about a work published in Poland, but first published in France, entitled: *Principes sur l'essence, la distinction et les limites des deux puissances spirituelle et temporelle, ouvrage posthume du père Laborde de l'Oratoire*. The author argued that the minister of the Church ought to submit himself to secular dominion. The secular can inspect the Church from the outside. It can know and judge of the external government of the Church. Benedict XIV responded, "This impudent author, under the verbal mask of piety and religion, forces treacherous forms of counterfeit reasoning in order to twist Scripture and the witness of the Fathers of the Church. He easily tricks simple readers with his false interpretations. And so this Apostolic See has rejected his destructive system as depraved as well and has expressly condemned it as heretical." Therefore, he characterized the book as deceptive, fraudulent, impious and heretical. He forbade each and every Christian from reading it, keeping it, or using it, even those who by right ought to have the qualities to read it. He excommunicated anyone who would read it and reserved to himself the right of absolution, except in the case of imminent death.

What reasonable amount of authority can the secular government exercise over the Church, or by what right should a minister of the Church submit to the decrees of a government? No Catholic can reasonably deny that, when Jesus Christ instituted his Church, he gave to his apostles and to their successors a power. This power cannot be beholden to any other power. All the Fathers of the Church, from Athanasius to Osio, give witness to the existence of this power. "Do not meddle in matters that have to do with the Church. Do not order us to accept your rules in the way that we do things. On the contrary, in these matters, you could learn something from us. God has given you the empire. But he has left the government of the Church in our hands. The one who tries in whatever way to take something in secret from you, revolts against the order of God. So too, you ought to fear that if you take by force what belongs to the Church, you yourself will commit a grave crime." And so, Saint John Chrysostom as if to verify this teaching as the truth, cited the example of Oza. He touched the Ark "to keep it from turning upside down, and he was dead in his tracks. It was not right for him to take for himself this ministry. He provoked the displeasure of God when he violated the Sabbath, even though he only touched the Ark of the Covenant. One might suppose that this was a small fault. How much more will those who corrupt our highly reverenced and sacred dogmas provoke the displeasure of God,? They do not have the excuse of committing a minor fault. You rightly agree with me. There is no excuse." Our Holy Councils use the same language. All the monarchs of France, including Louis XV, have assented to this doctrine. On 10 August 1731 he declared: "The first duty of our office is to hinder the occasion of disputes. We should not call into question the holy rights that God has granted: to judge questions of faith or the regulation of morals; to pass canon laws or disciplinary measures for governing the ministers of the Church, along with the faithful in their religious lives; to ordain ministers or to remove them from office; to lead the faithful to obedience to God by applying canonical norms that impose salutary penances as well as spiritual punishments; to give censures or punishments that spiritual pastors have the right to give."

Despite these unequivocal teachings of the Church, the National Assembly, without right, has claimed for itself the powers of the Church. They have passed a number of serious laws that go against the discipline of the Church. They would like all the bishops and priests of France to become complicit in putting the decrees into effect. But no one should be surprised to see this happening. It is a necessary effect of the constitutional decrees that the National Assembly has passed. They have the effect of abolishing the Catholic religion, and along with that, the obedience that citizens owe to the King. The Assembly has made this into a right: that Man, having agreed to enter into society, nevertheless enjoys unrestrained freedom. He should not be troubled at all in religious matters. He is the authority when it comes to judging the evidence for his religion. He can think, can say, can write, and can make public any image he wishes, especially in matters of religion. This makes evident the monster that follows from the equality of men with each other, and what can be derived from natural liberty. It is insane to think that we ought to establish this extreme equality and freedom among all men. It does not stand up to reason, the best gift that nature has given to human beings, and that which distinguishes him from beasts. When God created man, and placed him in the Garden of Delights, he announced that he would not suffer the pain of death unless he ate of the Tree of the Knowledge of Good and Evil. This first precept limits liberty. Afterwards, when his disobedience made him guilty, God added more limits through the Law of Moses. It is true that he has left him in the hand of his counsel, so that he can merit good or evil. Nevertheless, he has given commandments and precepts, so that if a man chooses to follow them, these will keep him safe.

Where, therefore, is this freedom of thinking and acting, which the decrees of the National Assembly grant to Man, constituted in society, as if this were an immutable natural right? It necessarily follows that the meaning of these decrees contradicts the rights of God the Creator. We exist because of Him. We are what we are and we have what we have because of his liberality. We ought to return what we have received. In addition, no one can ignore the fact that He has not created Man to live alone and for himself, but that he might live with other men and do good to them. The weakness of men in nature is such that they stand in need of mutual help. For this reason, God gave men the faculties of speech and reason so that they would be able to ask for help, and so that they might become responsible for those who seek their help. Therefore, nature herself unites men together in society and in community. Now Man profits from his reason not only when he recognizes God as his sovereign author, but also when he in truth worships Him, when he falls into a state of wonder before Him. He ought to give everything back to Him. In order to do this, he begins in the first stage of life by submitting himself to those who are older than himself. They guide him and teach him so that the use of reason as well as the standards of human nature and religion will be firmly fixed in his life. It is certainly the case that from the moment that the words liberty and equality rose up and were tossed into society that what they offered was empty and void. *By necessity be subject to authority.* Therefore, so that men may grow strong in civil society, they should put in place some form of government. This government draws the limits of the right of liberty, and men are rightly under its laws and the high authority of the rulers. It follows that, as Augustine teaches in these words, "a general requirement for the covenant that binds society together is that men obey their rulers." This power does not come from a social contract. It is derived from God, the Author of virtue and right. The Apostle Paul confirms this, "Let every soul be subject to higher powers, for there is no power but that which comes from God; and those who possess such power are ordained by God. Therefore, he who resists this power, resists the ordinance of God. And those who resist purchase to themselves damnation."

We refer here to the Second Council of Tours, from the year 567. They deemed anathema not only those who presumed to contradict the decrees of the Holy See, but also "worse, he who contradicts what is meant; that Paul, a vessel of election, had promulgated something other, meant to write something other or mean something other than what he said through the Holy Spirit, that he preached something other than what he preached, let him be anathema."

But, in order to refute the most absurd falsehood of this so called liberty, it is enough to point out that this so called liberty is the same liberty that the Waldensians and Beguines taught. Clement V, with the agreement of the ecumenical Council of Vienne, condemned this teaching. Thereafter, the followers of Wycliffe and then those of Luther made these words their own: "we are free from every constraint." Notwithstanding, we affirm the obedience that is owed to legitimate authority. We do not want to give the sense that we are opposed in principle to new civil laws, to which it is the King's responsibility to assent. Inasmuch as matters refer to how to run his regime, and if these matters were presented to us for our opinion, we would encourage him to restore matters to the former civil conditions. This would most likely be given a calumnious interpretation by those who burn with envy against religion, when in fact you and I are only seeking one thing, and we urge you to this task: to preserve the sacred rights of the Church and of the Apostolic See. For the purpose of better understanding this reasonable end, let us consider the word "liberty" making use of another point of view. We shall distinguish between what happens among men who are outside of the Church, infidels and Jews, and those who have received baptism and are now part of the Church. The obedience required of Catholics does not bind the former, but it does bind the latter. This is a meaningful distinction. Saint Thomas Aquinas explains why this is so. Many centuries earlier Tertullian explained why in his book *Adversus Gnosticos Scorpiace*. Just a few years ago, Benedict XIV acknowledged it in his work on beatification and canonization. But perhaps no one has offered a better argument on this point than Saint Augustine in two celebrated and often printed letters, one to Vincent, the Bishop of Cartagena, and another to Count Boniface. In these letters he fully refutes errors both ancient and modern. Now, it is clearly seen that the equality and liberty that the National Assembly has created, as we just showed, cuts down and subverts the Catholic religion. It does this because it has refused to give her the predominant title that she should always have in the realm.

We now turn to show other errors in the decrees of the National Assembly. First, they have abolished the primacy of the Pope in jurisdictional matters of the Church. They have established by decree that "the new bishop does not need to turn to the Pope in order to be confirmed. He must simply write to the Pope as the head of the universal Church. By doing this, he gives sufficient witness to the unity of faith and communion." They have prescribed a new formula for the Oath of Loyalty of a bishop that suppresses the name of the Roman Pontiff. What is more, the elected bishop swears to a kind of faith in the decrees of the National Assembly that restrains him. He does not request confirmation of his election from the Pope. Indeed, it cuts off any relationship of authority between the Pope and the bishop. It is as if they were attempting to cut off the streams from the river, the branches from the trunk, and the people from their first priest (the Vicar of Christ).

In order to deplore the attack on the dignity and the injustice done to the authority of the Pope, we borrow from the words of Saint Gregory the Great, who expressed his pain to the Empress Constantina when a certain bishop John, because of his pride, had taken to calling himself the universal bishop. Gregory prayed that he might give up this arrogant position: "In this case, may your piety not lead you to despise me. Certainly, it is the case that the sins of Gregory (we might apply these words to our self and say Pius VI) are so great, that he should suffer in this way. But it is not the case that the Apostle Peter has sinned in your times. And so, Peter should not suffer in this way. Therefore, through the power of the Omnipotent Lord, I ask you again and again, just as your princely ancestors before you sought the mercy of Saint Peter the Apostle: that you too take it upon yourself to seek this mercy and to keep yourself in its presence. We acknowledge that we have many sins and are his unworthy servant, but do not let our sins lessen in any way the honor that you have for him. He is now your true helper in all things. And when you die, he wishes to forgive your sins."

We now make to you the same request to uphold the papal dignity that Saint Gregory the Great made to the Empress Constantina. Do not let the Assembly abolish the honor and rights of the Papal Primacy in this vast Empire. Help them to have respect for the sacrifices of Peter. To be sure, we are his unworthy heir. Inasmuch as we represent him, we ought to be honored. Inasmuch as I am a human being, I ought to be humble. Be strong. Do not let a power outside the Church prevent you from carrying out your responsibilities. Fill yourselves with piety and constancy, in order to have the fortitude to abstain from taking the Oath of Loyalty that they are forcing on you. The offense of John, claiming the name of universal bishop, was a small harm against Gregory. By comparison, the Oath required by the National Decree is a major offense against us. By taking it, a bishop cannot realistically keep his communion with the visible head of the Church. Simply giving notice of one's election is no way of fostering unity. This is especially the case because, at the same time, the decrees require an oath in which the potential bishop or priest denies the spiritual authority that is attached to the Papacy. Canon law requires that every member of the hierarchy of the Church promise obedience to the Pope as the spiritual head of the Church. This is a basic requirement of unity in the Church. It prevents the mystical body of Christ from falling into schism. This is a matter that the Gallican Church has always recognized, as one can see in the *Ancient Ecclesiatical Rights* of Martenne. There is an oath that has been part of the ordination ceremony of bishops in France from ancient times. After making the profession of faith, the bishop concludes with a promise of obedience to the Roman Pontiff.

We are fully aware. We are unveiling the mask. The partisans of the National Constitution oppose our teaching. They make use of the letter of Saint Hormisdas to Epiphanius of Constantinople. It would be better said the distorted views that they draw from this letter, because in that letter one can see the custom by which they sought to obtain approval for their election. They sent to the Roman Pontiff delegates with letters and with their profession of faith. In these letters, they asked that they might be joined together in unity, as well as open communication with the Apostolic See. Epiphanius had failed to follow these procedures. And so, Hormisdas wrote to him, "I am surprised that you failed to follow the ancient customs that, God willing, bring about concord between the Churches. The duties of your office urgently demand that you seek full fraternity and peace. They do not instruct you to assert your personal arrogance. Instead, they tell you to follow what good example has established. It would have been fitting for you, my dear brother, at the beginning of your pontificate, to send delegates to the Apostolic See, so that we could show you our affection. You know well that this is the way that you must fulfill the ancient customs."

The adversaries of papal primacy contend that when the Pope used the verb "decuerat" ("it would have been fitting"), he meant to say that the delegate from Epiphanius to the Pope was an unnecessary courtesy, a ceremonial form without meaning. But from the context of the letter and from the words themselves, "reparata ecclesiarum...concordia...id flagitabat officium, quod...regularum observantia vindicabat...ut...vetustae consuetudinis formam rite compleres" ("to fulfill the duties prescribed by the rule in order to conform to the ancient custom"), we clearly see that by the word "decuerat" the pope simply wished to speak moderately. He did not want to convey in any sense that elected bishops did not need to seek his approval. If we look at the letter of Pope Saint Leo IX to Peter the bishop of Antioch, then we can definitively reject the interpretation that opposes our own. Peter had announced his election as bishop to the Holy Pontiff, to which the Pope replied: "We heartily support your effort to make a public announcement to me of your election. ..., it is of great credit to you and to the church over which you will govern for a time that you have not put this off. We say this with all humility, recognizing that we have been raised to the top apostolic throne to approve what merits approval, and to reject what ought to be rejected. With pleasure we approve, praise and confirm your promotion to the very holy fraternity of bishops. May the communion of the Lord pressingly prevail upon you. We also pray that what you have just said with human lips, may exist in truth before his eyes." This letter is not the speculation of a private theologian, but the judgment of a saintly Pontiff known for his knowledge of doctrine. He leaves no doubt as to the meaning that we have given to the letter of Saint Hormisdas. We should recognize it as an authentic witness to the rights of the Roman Pontiff to confirm the election of bishops. This right is further explained in the Council of Trent. We have further explained it in our response to nuncios. Many of you have explained it in your own learned writings.

But our adversaries, when defending the decrees of the National Assembly, argue that they only affect the discipline of the Church. Discipline can change from time to time according to the circumstances. And so, it can be changed in our day. But we have just shown that, although the decrees affect discipline, they do not only affect discipline. There are many other decrees that taken together destroy pure and immutable dogmas. But, if we limit our discussion to discipline, nowhere has it been known among Catholics for laymen to unilaterally change ecclesiastical discipline. Even Peter de Marca acknowledged that "when considering liturgical rites, ceremonies, sacraments, clerical censures, conditions of ministry, and discipline, the canons of Councils and decrees of the Roman Pontiffs are authoritative. This is the area of their competence and their jurisdiction. It would be difficult to refer to any aspect of the government of princes that would, in these matters, suggest unadulterated authority to the secular power. We see that in this part public laws have followed. There is no precedent to the contrary."

In 1560, the faculty of Paris examined the lawyer of the King, Francis Grimaudet. They brought him before the Estates assembled at Angers. Among a number of propositions that they found worthy of censure, we can point to this one found in number 6: "The second point of religion is in the government and discipline of priests. Princes and Kings have the power of passing statutes over them, ordaining them, and reforming them when they have become corrupted." This position is false, schismatic, and heretical. Its real purpose is to weaken ecclesiastical power. There are no convincing arguments for this position. At the same time, it is certain that discipline cannot be changed without a plan and by arbitrary will. The two greatest lights of the Church, Saint Augustine and Saint Thomas teach that discipline cannot be changed only when there is necessity, or because of great usefulness. But changes should be rare because the usefulness of good customs is often destroyed by novelty. Therefore, one should not change, according to Saint Thomas, "unless one part of the common good is built up, in exchange for that part of the common good which is modified." In general, the Roman Pontiffs shy away from changing discipline because they want to avoid corrupting discipline. Instead, they seek to use the authority that God has given them to work to build up the Church, to make it better and to perfect it. To our great sorrow, the National Assembly has done the opposite. One can easily see this by comparing any of the articles of the decrees with the actual disciplinary practice of the Church.

But before we touch on these articles, perhaps it would be good to show how much discipline is united to dogma and how it helps preserve its purity. Not only that: the few times that the Roman Pontiffs have allowed for a short period of time variation out of indulgence have never brought about the expected usefulness. Certainly, sacred Councils have in many cases excommunicated even those who violated only discipline. The Council of Constantinople in 692 excommunicated those who ate the blood of choked animals: "Hereafter, let no one attempt to eat the blood of animals. If he is a cleric, he shall be deposed. If he is a layman, he will be separated." In many places, the Council of Trent also put under anathema those who attacked the discipline of the Church. Canon 9, session 13, *On the Eucharist* imposes the penalty of anathema on anyone who "denies that every Christian faithful of either sex, upon arriving at the age of reason, is obliged to receive communion at least one time each year during the Pascal Season, according to the precept of the Holy Mother Church." Canon 7, session 22, *On the Sacrifice of the Mass*, renders anathema those who "say that that the ceremonies, vestments, and external signs that the Church uses during the Holy Mass are more likely to arouse the sarcasm of the impious than the piety of Christians." Canon 9 of the same session renders anathema those who assert "that the rite of the Roman Church is somehow at fault because it recommends that parts of the Mass and the words of the consecration be said in a low voice. In addition, it anathematizes those who say that the Mass ought to be celebrated in the vernacular language in a way that all can easily understand." Canon 4, session 24, *On the Sacrament of Marriage*, renders anathema those who say that "the Church is not able to establish the circumstances for declaring an impediment to marriage or the conditions for a valid marriage." Canon 9 renders anathema those who "say that clerics who have received Holy Orders, or religious who have professed solemn vows of chastity, can be married and that their marriage is valid, despite the laws of the Church or the reality of their vows. The only other possible position would be to condemn the institution of marriage itself. Finally, let him be anathema who claims that those, who, despite taking a vow of chastity, do not believe that they received the grace of chastity, can be married." Canon 11 likewise anathematizes those who say "the act of prohibiting nuptial ceremonies during certain times of the year is a tyrannical act propagating the superstition of the ethnic nations. In addition, they suggest that benedictions and other ceremonies that the Church employs are pagan superstitions." Canon 12 anathematizes those who say "there should not be ecclesiastical courts for marriage cases." Alexander VII on 7 January and 7 February 1661 placed under excommunication *latae sententiae*, those who published a version of the Roman Missal in French. This was a novelty that would deform the eternal beauty of the Church. It would initiate a spirit of disobedience, thoughtlessness, insolence, sedition, and schism in the Church. Many more evils would without difficulty follow from these.

Having reviewed these matters in which the Church levied anathemas against those who opposed her discipline, we can now clearly see that she has rightly made a connection between discipline and dogma. Discipline should not be changed without the approval of the proper ecclesiastical authority. The Church determines what usages should always stand and their purpose. She determines what should be ceded under necessity in order to preserve the common good.

It remains to be shown that often enough the advantages that were hoped for from changes did not come to pass, and so they did not remain. This is easily made clear if you remember the example of the use of the Chalice. The Emperor Ferdinand and Albert the Duke of Bavaria had urgently requested Pius IV to permit communion under both species in some dioceses of Germany and only under certain conditions. But Pius V saw that it brought more evil than good to the Church. At the beginning of his pontificate necessity led him to revoke these concessions in two apostolic letters, one on 8 June 1566, to John the Patriarch of Aquila, the second 9 June to Charles the Archduke of Austria. The Bishop of

Passau, Urban, had asked Pius V for the same concession. On 26 May 1568, Pius responded to him and strongly urged him to remain constant. He said, "It is better to preserve in tact the most ancient rites of the Catholic Church than to adopt the rituals of heretics. ... and you ought to persist in these teachings with constancy and fortitude. Neither the threat of losing some goods nor the fear of suffering some dangers should move you to deviate. You should be willing to sacrifice your goods and even to suffer martyrdom. You ought to prefer the good of such constancy to all the goods and all the riches of the world. Someone who is a true Catholic should not flee from martyrdom. It is expected of the one to whom God sends it. It is a rare gift. You ought to be happy if you find yourself worthy to give your blood in defense of Christ and of his Holy Sacraments." Saint Leo the Great had good reason to write about certain articles of discipline to the bishops of Campania, Picenum, and Tuscany. "If any brother attempts to come out against what has been established, or dares to allow for what has been prohibited, then he will be removed from his office and from being a future partner in our communion. This is because he does not wish to accept our discipline."

Now, if we turn and examine the various parts of the decrees that the National Assembly has passed, it did great harm when it suppressed an ancient metropolitan and several dioceses. It divided other dioceses and erected new ones. We do not intend to critically examine the history of ancient France in order to show beyond a doubt that it is not necessary that ecclesiastical organization map onto the political organization of the provinces according to time and circumstance. In this case it is enough to say that the jurisdiction of civil power is not the rule for determining the proper sphere of ecclesiastical ministry. Saint Innocent I gave good reason for this position: "After the Emperor divides the province into two jurisdictions, one may wonder whether there will be two metropolitans and whether we will have to name two metropolitan bishops. But the Church of God should not necessarily change because necessity requires the worldly to change. The Emperor changes the rules for honors and offices and to carry out his plans, but they should be patient in determining honors and ecclesiastical provinces. It follows that the metropolitan bishops should be named following the way that the ancient provinces were set out." Pierre de Marca appeals to the great example of the Church in France. It will only take a few words to convey his meaning: "The Gallican Church holds the same doctrine as the Council of Chalcedon and the decrees of Innocent. It is contrary to Divine Law for the King to command the institution of new bishops, etc. There is no good reason to depart from the common sense of the Universal Church and resort to the foul flattery of princes. Marco Antonio de Dominis argues against these canons when he maintains that Kings have the power to erect dioceses. Some modern interpreters have adopted his opinions, but, as I have just stated, sound reason leads one to hold that the Church possesses the authority to govern these matters."

They say that they have asked us to approve the Constitutional Decrees that divide the dioceses. If we were to give them only their due consideration, we would approve them. But the principles of the decrees seem defective if they lead to the proposed suppression and division of dioceses. But, we should be clear: in reality, we are not dealing with a change here or there in one or two dioceses. We are dealing with an attempt to destroy the life of the Church in every diocese of the Empire. It is about removing the veneration given to a host of Churches. The sign of this is that they take several long respected and exemplary archdioceses and they lower them to the level of dioceses. Innocent III sharply corrected this novelty in the way that we corrected the Patriarch of Antioch: "You have committed an offensive change. You have taken a greater diocese and made it smaller. You have taken a smaller diocese and made it bigger. When you make an archbishop into a bishop, this seems to be a form of degradation."

Yves of Chartres thought this novelty such a great matter that it was necessary to write to Pope Paschal II, and urge him not to let things be changed. He argued: "the Churches have been ordered in this way for at least 400 years. To leave this alone will prevent the disruption of order. It will help France to avoid any schisms against the Apostolic See like those that have arisen in Germany." We ought to add that, before coming to any decision in these matters, we ought to consult the bishop who will be affected by the decision. He also has rights. And we would be wrong to act against justice in these matters. See how much Pope Innocent I denounced similar conduct: "It is difficult to support those who overturn the established order, especially when those who are subverting things are the same ones who have the responsibility for keeping tranquility, peace, and concord. Now, we are seeing customs subverted. The leaders drive innocent priests and bishops from their positions. John, your bishop, as well as my brother and colleague in the priesthood, has been the first to suffer this injustice. No one gave him a reason for his dismissal. He did not commit a crime. There were no accusers. What kind of hopeless court has done this? It did not even seek to follow any procedure when making its judgment. They should be judged as either acting well or poorly in having thrown out the priest. They have used the courts to remove a priest while alive and to give his position to someone else. By judging in this way, they have committed a crime. We cannot find any example of this way of acting among our Fathers. Instead, we see them forbidding this kind of behavior. They would never permit a priest to take the place of a living bishop. The illegitimate consecration of a bishop cannot destroy the rights of the living bishop who is already in that place. The illegitimate bishop is not able to preserve intact the dignity of the priesthood. The unjust substitute cannot, in any way, be a bishop." Finally, before acting, we should be more informed about what the people think. Especially those who might be deprived of some good, that is, the loss of their pastor and the good services he offers his people.

Now, this change, or, better said, this subversion of discipline, has another consequence in the way we elect bishops. It breaks and violates the solemn agreement made between Pope Leo X and King Francis I and approved by the Fifth Lateran Council. They faithfully promised fidelity for 250 years. This was subsequently made part of the laws of France. When we look at the articles of the concordat, we see that it provides a mechanism for conferring bishoprics, prelatures, abbeys and benefices. Disregarding that law, the National Assembly has decreed that from now on the people in their districts and municipalities will elect their bishops. By acting in this way, the National Assembly wants to embrace the false opinions of Luther and Calvin. The apostate of Spalatro followed their lead. These three assert that Divine Right grants to the people the power to elect bishops. It is easy to find the error in this position. We only have to recall how bishops of old were elected. We shall begin with Moses. He made Aaron and then Eleazar priests without suffrage or any consultation of the people. Then, Christ, Our

Lord, chose the Twelve and then the seventy two disciples without any election. The holy apostle Paul ordained with his own hands Timothy at Ephesus, Titus on Crete and Dionysios the Areopagite at Corinth. Saint John made Polycarp the bishop of Smyrna without any consent of the governed. The Holy Apostles founded many Churches among the unfaithful in Pontus, Galatia, Cappadocia, Asia and Bithynia. Without consulting the people, they sent them an uncountable number of bishops to govern them. The First Lateran Council and the Fourth Council of Constantinople affirmed that these modes of selection were true to form. Saint Athanasius, while presiding over a council of priests made Frumentius the bishop of Indes, and the people were purposefully left out. During a synod, Saint Basil elected Euphronius as bishop of Nicopolitanus without any consent of the governed or petitioning of the populace. Gregory II ordained Saint Boniface as bishop in Germany. The Germans knew nothing about this and they did not care to know. The Emperor Valentinus Augustus responded to the bishops, when they were hoping to defer to him the task of choosing a bishop for Milan: "This choice is beyond my authority to make. You who have the grace of God, and who are able to discern his will, you are better electors." What Valentinus sensed, the legislators in France should come to learn, and all Catholic politicians should follow all the more.

In order to oppose the partisans of the decrees who enlist Luther and Calvin to support their position, we can point to Saint Peter who stood in the midst of 120 disciples and said: "We must choose from among these disciples, who have accompanied us, one who will be able to fulfill the ministry of Judas who rendered himself unworthy." Their reasoning is false. Peter did not grant the assembly the freedom to choose whoever they wished. Instead, he appointed and elected one from those men who were gathered together with him. Saint Chrysostom squelches any kind of strained interpretation when he says: "Who questions whether Peter himself has the power to elect? Without a doubt, he has the power. But he holds back and does not act out of self-interest." This is further confirmed by the subsequent actions of Peter, as Saint Innocent I explains in his letter to Eugubinum. As soon as the Arians obtained the special protection of the Emperor Constance, they began to use violence to chase the Catholic bishops from their offices.

They then put Arian bishops in those offices. Saint Athanasius deplored this injustice. The circumstances became such that he had recourse to the popular election of bishops as a way of assuring that the validly elected bishop would be able to keep in his office. But the hierarchy did not lose the right of election. This right has always been their unique right. Never has it not been recognized, and it has never been seriously contested. The people have never been given the sole power to elect bishops. The Roman Pontiffs have never abandoned this manner of exercising their authority. For example, Saint Gregory the Great sent the subdeacon John to Genoa, where many Milanese had assembled, so that he might learn their opinions concerning Constance. He did this so that if they all favored Constance, the bishops, with the approval of the Pope, would install him as the bishop of Milan. Again, in a letter addressed to the bishops in Dalmatia, he explained that, by the authority of Saint Peter, the Prince of the apostles, he did not need the consent of anyone or the permission of anyone to install a bishop in the city of Salone. He had the right to give this city the candidate that he designated. If they disobeyed, they would be prevented from celebrating the Mass on Sunday. He would approve the candidate, and the one that they installed would not be the legitimate bishop. In a letter to Peter, the bishop of Orante, he asks him to visit the cities of Brindes, Lupia, and Gallipoli. The bishops there had died. He would then find several priests who worthily carried out their ministry and recommend them to the Pope, so that he could consecrate them as bishops. Then, in a letter to the people of Milan, he approved the choice of Dieudonné to replace Constance. Then recommends that, if there are no canonical impediments, he allows him to be ordained by his solemn authority. Saint Nicholas I did not hesitate to correct King Lothar when he tried to establish bishops in his realm that he could easily control. He ordered, by the authority of his Apostolic position as well as by Divine Witness, that Lothar should consult the Apostolic See before establishing bishops at Trèves and Cologne. Innocent III annulled the election of the bishop of Penna, because he had the audacity to sit upon the episcopal throne before he was called or confirmed by the Roman Pontiff. Likewise, he deposed Conrad as Bishop of Hildensheim and Wirtzburg, because Conrad attempted to take control of both dioceses without the approval of the Pope. Saint Bernard humbly asked Honorius II that he deign to raise Alberic to the bishop of Châlons-sur-Marne. This deed makes clear that the holy abbot knew that the election of a bishop was negated if it did not receive the approval of the Pope.

Finally, the see constant discord, tumult, and so many other abuses make it proper to remove the people from having influence in elections. We should refrain from consulting their witness and their personal desires when electing bishops.

If we look at history, we can see that the Popes excluded Catholic laypeople from electing bishops. Even more so now, the National Assembly should not have a role electing bishops in France. That same Assembly, among whose ranks one can see Jews, heretics, and all kinds of heterodox people, has forced clerics to give up their habit. Saint Gregory the Great did not wish this to happen. He saw that such a group would not be indifferent in the election of bishops. And he rightly detested what would follow from their influence. He wrote to the people of Milan: "We are never able to grant our rational consent to a man who not only is not chosen by Catholics, but also has been elected by the Lombards. If such a man were to be elected and then ordained, he would be an unworthy successor to Saint Ambrose."

The democratic way of electing bishops would renew all sorts of perturbations. It would bring back offensive behaviors that have been abolished for so long. It would be too easy for men to select bishops who would share their errors and teachers who would probably foster sentiments in agreement with those who elected them. And so, Saint Jerome warned Christians: "Often the people err in making a judgment. When choosing a priest, each one would like to choose the man who confirms his prejudices. He does not seek the good pastor, but the one who is most like himself." What can we expect from bishops who have entered through another door? Certainly, we ought to fear the evil that these men could work against religion. They themselves are caught in the vice of error. They, therefore, will by no means be able to free the people from error. Without question, pastors of this sort will have no power to bind and loose, seeing that they will lack a legitimate mandate. The Holy See will immediately declare them to be outside the communion of the Church. This is the penalty that has always been applied in these circumstances. This was most recently done by a public announcement against all bishops illegitimately elected in Utrecht.

Something even worse logically follows if one understands the spirit of these decrees. Namely, once a department has elected a bishop, the candidate is ordered to go to the metropolitan or to the oldest bishop in order to obtain his confirmation as bishop. If the authority refuses, he is obliged to put down in writing the reasons for his refusal. Those who are denied their positions are able to then go to the civil magistrates and claim that an abuse has been committed. The magistrates will have greater authority than the metropolitan to judge whether an abuse has been committed. Thus, by indirectly trumping the power of the bishops to judge, the decrees are denying them their legitimate authority to judge matters of morals and doctrine. They also deny bishops the task that they have according to Saint Jerome – that of protecting the people from error. But something makes even clearer not only the illegitimacy, but also the incompetence of this appeal to the laity. Let us recall the memorable example of the Emperor Constantine. Many bishops had gathered together at Nicaea to hold a Council. Several thought that the Emperor ought to attend this Council. With the Emperor present, they could denounce the Arians to him. After he read the requests that were sent to him, the Emperor responded: "I am just a man. It would be inappropriate for me to claim to know as fully as a priest which people are accused and which are accusing." We could provide many more examples of this kind. But we choose not to do so, because we think the point is clear. One can simply juxtapose the behavior of Constantine with that of his son Constance. Constance declared himself an enemy of the Catholic Church and claimed for himself the same power that his father had denied himself. I cite the witness of Saint Athanasius and Saint Jerome, who both railed against this sacrilegious abuse of authority.

The goal of the decrees that the Assembly has passed is clear. It hopes to diminish and then reduce to nothing the episcopate in France. It possesses a hatred for the Catholic religion, and the bishops, as the representatives of that religion, will feel the effects of that hatred. One can see this goal because the Assembly has established a permanent council of priests that they call vicars. In cities of more than 1,000 inhabitants, there are sixteen members per council. In cities of fewer people, the number is reduced to twelve. The bishops are forced to attach priests whose parishes have been suppressed to themselves. They are called vicars *pleni juris*, and, by the force of this right, they are not subject in obedience to the bishops to whom they are attached. While the bishop is left free to choose some vicars, they are nevertheless prohibited from taking any jurisdictional action without their approval (any act would be provisional). The vicars chosen by the bishop could also be removed by a plurality of votes on the council. What we seem to have here are the conditions under which priests will rule in the diocese and will overthrow the authority of the bishop. This way of acting contradicts the doctrine which can be read in the Acts of the Apostles: "the Holy Ghost has chosen you as bishops to rule over the Church of God, which he has purchased with his own blood." But now, the whole order of the sacred hierarchy is shaken and turned on its head. Priests take on the same equality as bishops. As Benedict XIV shows in his *Work on the Diocesan Synod*, Aerius first taught this error, then Wycliffe, then Marsilius of Padua, then Jean of Jandun, and finally Calvin.

There is more. The priests are given a place of authority before the bishop. The bishop cannot remove them from the council and the bishop cannot decide anything without a plurality of votes from his vicars. Nevertheless there are already canonical councils that can exist in the Church and they function somewhat like a senate. The bishop can call them together and they can offer a consultative vote to the bishop, as Benedict XIV decreed after two provincial councils in Burgundy.

But if we consider the role of these other vicars, the vicars *pleni juris*, it is very strange – almost unheard of – that bishops would have to accept their work, even when they have just cause for rejecting them. It is also absurd that those who carry out subordinate functions in the government of the diocese take the place of the man under whom they supposedly work.

Let us proceed. The Assembly has left to the bishop the power to choose his personal vicars from among the clergy. But, when it comes to regulating seminaries, the Assembly has decreed that he can only choose a director for the seminary based on the vote of the council of vicars, and he can only remove the head of the seminary if he obtains a plurality of votes among the vicars. This point is an act of defiance against the bishops. It is the bishops who are charged by their institution with enforcing discipline over those who may be admitted into the diocese and employed in its ministry. It is undeniable that the bishop is the highest administrator and head of the seminary. Furthermore, the Council of Trent commands that two canons oversee the ecclesiastical formation of seminarians. At the same time, it mandates that the bishop choose those two directors, as the Holy Spirit inspires him. He is under no compulsion to conform to their judgments or assent to their counsels. It is very likely that bishops will not be able to have much trust in priests who are chosen by some other entity, especially if they are chosen by men who have sworn an oath to restrict the faith and to preserve the poisonous decrees passed by the National Assembly.

Finally, the ultimate act by which the Assembly has turned the bishops into extreme outsiders and holds them in the utmost contempt is the act by which the Assembly allows the bishops every three months to receive a stipend, as if they were mercenaries. They can no longer relieve the hardships of the indigent, which make a great part of this realm suffer. Nor can they maintain episcopal dignity. This new institution of a stipend for bishops opposes ancient laws. These laws allow for bishops and priests to possess stable funds which they administer and of which they can enjoy the fruit. We see this in the laws that Charlemagne and Lothar passed: "We will, just as Our Lord willed, that each parish be given a domain with twelve *bunariis* of arable land." And if what is given proves to be insufficient to maintain the bishop, then one can join it together with the revenues of the local abbey, as has often been done in France – even under our pontificate, as we would like to recall. But now, the livelihood of the bishop depends entirely on the power of a group of secularized men. These men can refuse the bishop his salary if he opposes their perverse decrees. Now, because every bishop has a fixed salary, he can no longer help a suffragan or coadjutors, even if necessity requires it. It is no longer within his power to provide for those needs he sees it fit to provide for. Yet, we often see in a diocese that a bishop because of old age or bad health needs a coadjutor bishop. The archbishop of Lyon asked the Holy Father for a suffragan for this very reason, and he was paid out of the account of the archbishop.

We can all clearly see, beloved sons and venerable brothers, how these decrees reverse principal points of ecclesiastical discipline. Their suppressions, divisions, the creation of new episcopal sees, and the sacrilegious election of bishops can only result in a host of evils. For the same reason, one can see the evil lurking behind the suppression of parishes. You already noted this in your letter, but we would like to add our own reflections. The power that the administrators of the departments have granted themselves to establish the boundaries of parishes, as well as to suppress parishes as they deem fit, is extremely extraordinary and causes us a great anxiety. We are also disturbed that the National Assembly has decreed that in towns or villages of 6,000 inhabitants there can only be one parish. One parish priest is not enough for that many parishioners. Recall how Cardinal Conrad corrected a parish priest. Gregory IX sent the Cardinal to preside over a synod at Cologne. This priest had strongly opposed allowing brother preachers to enter into this city. The Cardinal asked him how many parishioners were in his parish. The priest told him 9,000. "Then you are quite unfortunate," responded the Cardinal, astonished and angry, "and who are you that you are able to instruct and lead so many thousands of men? Do you not know, blind and foolish as you are, that at the Day of Judgment you will have to answer before Christ's Tribunal for all the souls that have been entrusted to your care? And you are complaining that you might have as your vicars fervent religious, who will freely carry out the task that is entrusted to you. And so, because you wish me to prove to you that you are unworthy to govern a parish, I deprive you of your right to govern a parish." Of course, this passage refers to 9,000 parishioners. In comparison, the decree of the National Assembly assigns one priest to 6,000 parishioners. It is still the case, however, that it is beyond the capacity of one priest to provide adequate spiritual help to 6,000 parishioners. The decrees effectively deprive many parishioners of the spiritual help they need. We should not forget that they also suppress the religious orders.

For now, we pass over the invasion of ecclesiastical property in which the Assembly has followed the errors of Marsilius of Padua and Jean of Jandun, which have been condemned by John XXII. Many authors have also noted that Pope Saint Boniface I long before issued similar decrees. The Sixth Council of Toledo declared: "No one can licitly ignore that all things that are consecrated to God, whether a man, an animal, a field, or any thing, is to be considered holy. It has rights similar to that of the priesthood. Whoever tries to take, ravage, pillage or usurp what belongs to the Lord and his Church has committed a sacrilege, and he ought to expiate for his crime to the satisfaction of the Church. If he persists in his usurpation, he ought to be excommunicated." Loyse observes in his notes on the Council, letter D: "It is criminal to take or steal goods which the faithful in sincere faith have given to the Church. It would take up too much space to quote the writings of the many learned men who show this. I will simply add what one can read in the Eastern Constitutions. Nicephorus Phocas took the goods given to monasteries and churches. Moreover, he passed a law preventing the faithful from giving furniture to churches, under the pretext that the bishops would make poor use of the furniture, providing goods for the poor, while the army lacked what was necessary. Basil the Younger suppressed this impious and arrogant law and replaced it with a law that was more seemly. God has given to our empire monks proven in piety and virtue as well as other holy men. They argue that the laws of the usurper Nicephorus against the churches and religious houses are the root of the evils that afflict us. They are a source of universal subversion and confusion. They harm to the point of blood not only the churches and religious houses, but also strike at God himself. Experience proves their observations. Since these laws have been passed, we have not experienced any happiness. We have experienced a number of calamities. I am persuaded that my authority comes from God, and so I ordain by the present golden decree that as of today the people do not have a duty to follow the law of Nicophorus. In the future, his law is to be considered abolished and regarded as nul. The older laws with respect to the churches of God and religious houses should be re-established."

This example was ancient and constant throughout France, among the great men and was expressed in the desires of the French people. We see this in the prayers of Charlemagne in the year 803: "We bend our knees and beseech Your Majesty. Protect the bishops from the hostility that they have suffered until now. As we go out to meet the enemy, let them live peacefully in their parishes. We want you and all the kingdom to know that we do not want them to give anything unless it pleases them to give it. We do not wish to deprive them of their churches. But, if the Lord wishes it, we hope to see them grow, so that they, you and we all might be closer to salvation and so that God might better administer it. We know that the goods of the Church are consecrated to God. We know that they are offerings of all of the faithful to God. They are the price of our sins. We know that, if anyone takes the goods that the faithful have given and that have been consecrated to God from the churches, there is no doubt that he has committed a sacrilege. If a man does not see this reality, he is blind. When someone has given his goods to the Church, he has offered and dedicated them to God and to his saints, but to no one else. The actions and the words of the giver prove this. He writes down what goods he desires to give to God. He does this before the altar, and, taking into his hands what he has written, he says to the priests and to the guardians of the place: 'I offer to God and I dedicate all the goods which are described in this paper for the remission of my sins, and those of my parents and children. … If anyone takes these goods, after they have been offered in this way, he has committed a sacrilege. If he takes the goods of his friend, he is a thief. But to steal from the Church is undoubtedly a sacrilege. … And so that all of the goods of the Church may be preserved in the future without any fraud, either by your successors or ours, we ask you to place our request in the archives of the Church and to give it a place among your chapters.'"

The Emperor responded to these things as follows: "We grant what you have asked. … We know that many kingdoms and Kings have ceased to exist because they have despoiled the churches, ravaged their goods and sold them, alienated their property, or taken away their bishops, priests, and, what is worse, stolen their churches. So that these goods may be preserved with more respect in the future, we order the following instructions to be given, in our name and in the name of our successors, for as long as necessary, to all persons, whoever they may be; if anyone accepts or sells, under any pretext, the goods of the Church without the will and consent of the bishop of the dioceses in which the goods are situated, that man is a usurper of those goods. If this happens during our reign or the reign of one of our successors, that person has committed a crime, and he is subject to the same punishment as one who has committed a sacrilege. We, our successors, and our judges shall legally punish him as a murderer and a sacrilegious thief. Furthermore, the bishops should anathematize such a man."

Anyone who participates in this kind of usurpation should recall the punishment that the Lord gave to Heliodorus and his helpers. They tried to steal the goods of the Temple. The Spirit of the Lord gave evidence of his great omnipotence. All who dared to be there fell down before the power of God and were overcome with fear. A horse covered with wondrous harnesses along with the most wondrous rider appeared to them. The rider, who seemed to have arms made out of gold, attacked Heliodorus, striking his hands and feet. Two other young men appeared. They were beautifully dressed, with the splendor of virtue, bright and glorious. They stood on either side of Heliodorus and unceasingly whipped him, giving him innumerable wounds. Suddenly, Heliodorus fell to the ground, and darkness surrounded him. They took him away and placed him in a chair so that they could carry him. This can be read in II Maccabees 3:24-28. In that case, we were dealing with gold that was neither intended for the Temple sacrifice nor for the expenses of maintaining the Temple. It was gold that had been put aside as alms for the poor, for widows, and for orphans. Regardless, God inflicted a heavy punishment on Heliodorus and his companions because they violated the Majesty and Holiness of the Temple and they stole its goods. This example terrified Theodosius so much that he renounced his plan to take the treasure of a widow which had been deposited in the church of Pavia, according to Saint Ambrose.

More surprising still is that, while they are stealing the goods of the Church and the goods of priests, they protect the goods of Protestants who themselves have invaded the Church and rebelled against her. Of course, the Assembly has provided cover for this behavior. It seems that the National Assembly values treaties with protestants. It does not value canon law or agreements that the Holy See had made with Francis I, however. The Assembly seems to take pleasure in this, inasmuch as priests of God are brought to their ruin. It is not readily understood that taking the goods of the Church and profaning the temples will lead many to hold the ministers of the Church in contempt. This might turn many others from choosing to walk with the Lord. As of now, they have begun to seize the goods. They will not finish until divine worship is abolished, until the churches are closed, until the sacred vessels are taken, until choirs in churches no longer sing the Divine Office. France, since the sixth century, has had the great benefit of seeing chapters of clerks regular flourish in her bosom, as one can see from the authority of Gregory of Tours, in the mementos that Mabillon has assembled in his works on ancient relics and in the Third Council of Orléans, held in 538. But today, France weeps. The decrees of the National Assembly have unjustly and inhumanly dismantled many pious institutions. The first task of the canons was to sing each day the Psalms to praise God. Paul the Deacon shows this in his lives of the Bishops of Metz. "Bishop Chrodegand prepared his clergy not only to study the law of God, but he also took pains to teach them Roman Chant, and he encouraged them to conform the usage and practice of the Church in Rome." Charlemagne sent Pope Adrian I a work to review on *The Cult of Sacred Images*. The Pope took advantage of the occasion to encourage the Emperor to establish the use of chant in as many churches as possible in France. He was aware that some churches had for quite some time resisted following this practice of the Roman Church. However, the Pope argued that churches that saw the Roman Church as their rule and guide for the faith, should look at her in a similar way when it came to worshipping the Divinity. We see the response of Charlemagne in the work of George, *On the Liturgy of the Sovereign Pontiff*. As a result, the Emperor established a school of chant in the Monastery of Centule, following the model that Saint Gregory the Great had begun in Rome. He provided room and board for one hundred young men. They were divided into three classes and helped the monks in chanting hymns and psalms. Coloman Sanftl, the religious librarian of the Monastery of Saint Emmeran of Ratisbonne, has recently confirmed and solidified our understanding in a dissertation (dedicated to us) concerning an ancient and precious manuscript of the Gospels preserved in the monastery. "In the beginning, the bishops of Spain and France made great efforts to establish a uniform rite for the divine office among all the provinces. We come across various decrees to this effect in France and Spain. The most remarkable to this effect is the Council of Toledo IV, 531. The Fathers, after expounding the Catholic Faith, wished to establish a uniform method of chant for all the churches. One can see this goal put forth in the second Canon." Father Mabillon also speaks of the importance of the same usage in his research on Gallican Liturgy.

The Gallican Church has established, instructed, and preserved this rite through many centuries. It has given ecclesiastical canons a place of honor in society. They preserve and make available to the faithful a rite that nourishes their piety and raises their devotion. It invites them by the attraction of chant and the sound of the ceremonies, to contemplate Divine Mysteries and obtain the grace of reconciliation with God. The National Assembly has through one act given offense to nearly all involved, by suddenly annihilating, overturning, and abolishing the good that comes from chant. Just as with all of the other parts of the decree, they seem to follow the teachings of heretics. They imitate the wild ravings of Wycliffites, Centuriators of Magdeburg, and Calvinists against the ancient modes of singing in the Church, replacing them with debauched tones. Father Martin Gerbert, abbot of the monastery of Saint Blaise in the Dark Forest has written copiously against them. We had the opportunity to see this famous and illustrious author several times during the trip that we made to Vienna in 1782 on behalf of religion.

We must also consider the authors of the decrees of the Council of Arras, who in 1025 pronounced anathemas against the enemies of ecclesiastical chant in the hopes of moving them closer to Truth. "You cannot deny that you have adopted a worldly spirit and that you have rejected as a superstition the use of the psalmody that the Church has adopted under the guidance of the Holy Spirit. We need to remember that the Fathers of the Old and New Testaments, not the makers of public games and entertainment, prompted the Church to take up this way of singing. …Those who hold that the psalmody has nothing to do with divine cult should be thrown out of the bosom of the Church. … These thinkers feel the same way as their chief, the Devil, the Father of all Iniquity. He understands Sacred Scripture, but seeks to corrupt it through contorted and strained interpretations." And so, if the glory of the House of God and the majesty of divine worship becomes degraded, as a necessary consequence, the number of priests will decline. France will resemble Judea as Augustine describes her: "Because she lacked prophets, she fell into blindness just at the moment she was hoping for the time of her improvement."

We now come to clerks regular. The National Assembly has confiscated their goods. She has put them at the disposal of the Nation. The decree of 13 February, signed six days later by the king, suppresses all the religious orders and prevents anyone from founding a religious order in the future. This goes against all historical experience and what is necessary for the life of the Church. The Council of Trent gave witness to this fact when she declared: "This Sacred Synod cannot ignore how monasteries piously established and properly administered perfect the Church and give much glory to God."

The Fathers of the Church praised religious orders. Saint John Chrysostom, among others, wrote three letters against their detractors. Saint Gregory the Great warned Marinies, archbishop of Ravenna, to not become overly vexed against the monasteries. On the contrary, he ought to protect them and seek to bring together a great number of religious. He gathered together a large number of bishops and priests and issued a decree in which he indicated that no bishop or secular ruler should cause any harm to the goods or finances of religious houses, for whatever reasons. In the XIII Century, Guillaume of Saint-Amour in his book *On the Dangers of Our Times*, argued against those who would have men convert and then take on the religious life. But after reviewing this book, Alexander VI declared it prejudiced, harmful, abominable, and dangerous.

Two doctors of the Church, Saint Thomas and Saint Bonaventure, have also written against Guillaume. Luther embraced the same doctrine that was subsequently condemned by Leo X. The Council of Rouen, 1581, encouraged bishops to protect and cherish the orders of clerks regular, to share with them their tasks of ministry, to nourish them as if they were coadjutors, and to take upon themselves the insults and calumnies levied against them. History has also recorded the pious vows of Louis IX, King of France, who arranged to have two sons that he had during his expedition in the East raised in a monastery. When they had obtained the age of reason one joined the Dominicans. The other joined the Friars Minor. Both were formed in this holy school, which promoted the love both of religion and of the liberal arts. In addition, their father desired with all his heart that these young princes be formed with the most health-giving precepts and be inspired by the Spirit of God. They consecrated themselves fully to the life of piety in the monasteries in which they received their education. In our own days, the authors of the work entitled *Treatise on Contemporary Diplomacy* refute the enemies of the privileges granted to the religious. They do so with much energy: "We ought to pay close attention to the diatribes that the writers of public ecclesiastical history in France have made against the privileges granted to monasteries. One cannot take back these privileges and exemptions without subverting the hierarchy and violating the rights of the bishops. They are truly serious abuses. There is no right reason to rise up against a discipline that is so old and that is authorized within both the Church and the State."

Anyone who looks at the matter can see that several religious orders have become infected and have lost their initial fervor. The spirit that inspired their respective foundations has weakened. They have loosened their original discipline. These are not reasons to destroy the orders. Listen to how Jean de Polemar responded to the objections of Pierre Rayne at the Council of Bale. He admitted that the religious orders had slipped in their practices to such an extent that there was need of reform. "But in admitting that they need correction, along with the other Estates, we also recognize that the preaching and doctrine by which they illuminate the Church does not need reform. A prudent man who finds himself in a dark room would not put out all its light. If he sees sap or dross, he would be better served to clean it up. If he wants to clean it up, he would be better off making the light a little brighter rather than extinguishing it altogether." This passage is similar to that of Augustine, who said long ago: "Should we give up the study of medicine just because we are confronted with so many seemingly incurable diseases?"

To the contrary, the National Assembly abolished the religious orders, thereby acting in accordance with centuries of heretics, and prohibited the public profession of the evangelical counsels. She condemned as harmful a way of living commended by the Church for centuries. She claims that the holy founders of such institutions, whom we venerate on our altars, had no religious inspiration in doing what they did. By her decrees of 13 February 1790 the National Assembly no longer recognizes the reality of solemn religious vows. As a consequence, it also declares that any orders or religious congregations that have been founded on such vows should be suppressed in France, and to remain suppressed, never again to be restored in this country. In acting as it has, the Assembly has attempted to take on itself the ability to recognize or not the legitimacy of a vow, an exercise of authority that is reserved for the Roman Pontiff. Saint Thomas Aquinas states: "the great vows, that is, vows of chastity, etc., are reserved to the sovereign pontiff. These vows are contracted with God. They are solemnly made for our benefit, as is said in Psalm 75 verse 12: 'make a vow and pay homage to the Lord your God.' Also, in Ecclesiastes: 'If thou hast vowed anything to God, defer not to pay it: for an unfaithful and foolish promise displeases him: but whatsoever thou hast vowed, pay it.'"

Furthermore, the Sovereign Pontiff can make a judgment to dispense someone from solemn vows. He does not do this by means of his personal arbitrary power. It is something that proceeds from the manner in which the declaration is made. One should not be surprised that Martin Luther taught that we are not permitted to make vows to the Lord God. He was an apostate and had deserted his religious order. The members of the National Assembly wish to make it appear as though they consulted the people. They seem to know the murmurs and reproaches that will be made about their deeds once they are known, however. And so, they have also taken away the habits from the religious. They wish for no visual sign to remain of the vows that have been taken but are now repressed. They wish to suppress from the people's minds any memory of religious orders. By doing this, they will also suppress all that the religious orders did by protecting them from errors and keeping them from the corruption of morals. The Council of Sens knew how to recognize such perfidious and harmful deeds and it described them with energy: "They would grant to monks, and anyone who is bound by a vow, the freedom to follow their passions. They offer them the liberty to throw off their habits and to enter again into the world. They invite them to apostasy and teach them to oppose the decrees of Pontiffs and the canons expressed in Councils."

We also wish to add the following about the vows of clerks regular. The decrees do great harm to women who have taken vows as consecrated virgins. The Assembly, following the example of Luther, casts them out of their cloisters. As Hadrian VI described the heresiarch: "He shows no respect in the way that he stains the holy vessels of God. He throws virgins consecrated to God out of their convents and exposes them to the profane world. He seems to leave them to the devil." But the religious, a distinguished group among the Catholic flock, have often saved cities from the greatest dangers through their prayers. Gregory the Great admitted that, "if it were not for the religious who have lived in Rome among us for such a long time, we would not have escaped the sword of the Lombards." Benedict XIV gave a similar witness to the monks of Bologna. In it he said: "This city, which has been prone to so many calamities for so many years, would not be here today, if the prayers of the religious had not appeased the Wrath of Heaven." The religious of France are now subject to countless violent aggressions. We commiserate with them. Many of them have written to us from the several provinces of France to share their sufferings at not being able to follow their rules or properly fulfill their vows. They have indicated to us that they would prefer to suffer all things than to give up their vocation. Dear sons and venerable brothers, we now give witness to their faithfulness and courage, and we beseech you to help them with your counsel and teaching. Give them all of the help that you are able.

We could offer many more warnings about the Civil Constitution of the Clergy. From the beginning to the end it seems to be full of decrees that run from dangerous to reprehensible. But, in each of its parts, it seems to be motivated by the same spirit and the same principles. It seems that there is hardly one article that is preserved from error. However, we will now declare to you which is the most monstrous of all the errors in the decrees. While we were reviewing the most surprising articles of the decrees, we saw among the public papers of the Bishop of Autun, much to our surprise, the belief in the necessity of taking an oath of loyalty towards such a faulty constitution. We felt such a great sorrow that our pen fell from our hand. It took a great effort simply to continue our work. Day and night our eyes were filled with tears. We had just seen a bishop separate himself from his colleagues and make God a witness to his errors. To be sure, he offered a rationalization of the article that made a new distribution of dioceses. But his was a frivolous comparison, and it can only trick the simple and the ignorant. It is the same thing, he said, as if the people of a diocese were told by the civil authority to move to another diocese because of a public calamity or some other pressing need. But there is no parity between the two examples. When the people of one diocese leave it and move to another diocese, the bishop of the diocese in which they now live exercises proper and ordinary jurisdiction over them. Jurisdiction never passes to the civil power. It remains with the bishop of that place. It comes with his title. This is so because everyone who lives in a diocese must submit in accordance with justice to the bishop who governs the diocese. This is the case as long as they stay in or have a home in that place. If one can imagine the situation in which all the people of a diocese were to move out and leave the bishop absolutely alone, this shepherd without a flock would not be any less of a shepherd. His church would not be any less of a Cathedral. The bishop and the church would still keep all of their rights. This is what is the case for those churches that have fallen under the dominion of the Turks or of the infidels. On them we still often grant the title of bishop. But when the boundaries of the dioceses are entirely shaken and confused, when the dioceses are in whole or in part leveled and their bishop is exiled, even then the bishop is not allowed to abandon the flock entrusted to him, unless he is authorized to do so by the Church. And a bishop who has been given a diocese in an irregular way cannot exercise any authority over a place not legitimately entrusted to his care. Nor can he leave his flock to another pastor. This is so because the canonical mission and the jurisdiction of each bishop is delimited by certain boundaries. The civil authority has no right to expand them or to contract them.

It is difficult to think of a more insidious comparison than the one which equates moving to another diocese with the changes that the decrees propose for the limits of dioceses and for the administration of those dioceses. In the first case, the bishop cannot stop acting in his diocese, in accordance with the rights and responsibilities given to him. In the second case, the bishop attempts to extend his authority into a foreign diocese, where he has no right to exercise any authority. We fail to see anything contained in Catholic doctrine that could allow for the Oath of

Loyalty impiously taken by the Bishop of Autun. The first qualities that one should look for in an oath are those of Truth and Justice. But after the principles that we have reviewed, where is the Truth or the Justice in an oath that reinforces things that are false and illegitimate? The bishop of Autun cannot simply excuse himself with the claim that he acted in the heat of the moment and without reflection. His oath was the fruit of reflection and a premeditated plan. The proof of that is the fact that he has sought out sophisms to rationalize his deeds. During these many months, he has also seen the example of his colleagues, who have opposed this constitution with piety and wisdom. In addition, he must remember his ordination as a bishop. Should he not be able to discern the nature of an oath quite different than the one he took at this ceremony? It is necessary to conclude that he has fallen into voluntary, sacrilegious perjury. He has taken an oath against the dogma of the Church and has most certainly put himself in opposition to her legitimate rights.

At this moment, we should call to mind the example of what came to pass in England under the reign of Henry II. This King drafted a constitution of the clergy similar to that of the National Assembly, though there were fewer articles. He abolished the ancient rights of the English Church. He took upon himself the rights and the authority reserved for ecclesiastical authorities. He ordered his bishops to take an oath in which they promised to follow his constitution. He claimed that doing so would involve nothing more than confirming the ancient customs of the realm. The bishops did not refuse to take the oath. But, they did ask if they could include one additional clause: "except the rights of their order" (*salvo ordine suo*). The King was not pleased with this clause. He claimed that a virus was hidden within this clause. Instead, he would prefer that the bishops swear a simpler oath in order to conform to the ancient royal customs. When the King gave this dangerous response, the bishops of the country were in fear and dismayed. Thomas, the Archbishop of Canterbury, who afterwards died as a holy martyr, encouraged them to resist. This priest inflamed their courage and exhorted them to faithfully carry out their responsibilities as shepherds. "But as the days passed, the evils and sufferings of the Church grew and became more serious. Some bishops wrote to the Archbishop, petitioning him to give up his stubbornness lest he be imprisoned and lest the clergy suffer exile.

This man, one of unconquerable constancy to this very day, one founded on the rock of Christ, whom neither caresses nor threats could lead to grant concessions, moved by mercy for his clerics, and not for his own benefit, tore himself from the bosom of Truth and from the arms of his Mother." He took the oath. Other bishops followed his example. But the archbishop soon discovered his error. Filled with great sorrow, he breathed deeply and declared that he "repented, trembling in fear before his serious excesses: 'I am unworthy to exercise the ministry of the priesthood before the altars of Jesus Christ. I have too easily sold away the rights of the Church. I should sit in silence and remorse, waiting for the Grace of God to visit me to see if I may be found worthy to be absolved by the hand of the Pope. It is clear to me now what my sins have done. I ought to have supported the Church in England, that same Church that my predecessors prudently ruled amidst so many and such great dangers. They led the Church as generals lead an army into battle and thereby won many battles. Before me she emerged as Queen and Mother. Through me she has now been reduced to slavery. I would prefer never to have been born than to be associated with such deeds.'"

Thomas immediately wrote to the Pope. He revealed his wound and, seeking absolution, asked for the remedy. The Pope saw that Thomas had not taken the oath of his own will but through misguided piety. Moved by just mercy, the Pope absolved Thomas by virtue of the Papal Apostolic authority. Thomas received the letters from the Pope as though they came from heaven. He did not delay in admonishing the King. He did so agreeably, but remained firm in the essential matters. He also did everything in his power to prevent the prince from further harming the Church. In the meantime, the King had learned that Thomas had retracted his initial oath. He sent letters to the Pope asking him to grant two things: first, to approve what he called the ancient royal customs; second, to move the privilege of the legate of the Pope from Canterbury to York. The Pope rejected the first request. One sees this in his letter to Saint Thomas. He granted the second, because he could do so without harming the honor and the rights of the clergy. He then wrote to the bishop of York to warn him neither to carry out any act of jurisdiction within the province of Canterbury nor to bring his pectoral cross into that territory. Afterwards, Thomas had to flee to France and then to Rome where the Pope so humanly received him. Thomas showed the Pope the constitutions in sixteen articles, containing the ancient royal customs. The Pope reviewed them and rejected them. Then, the fearless Thomas, upon his return in England, went forward to his punishment remembering this divine precept: "Whoever wishes to come after me, he must deny himself, take up his cross and follow me." He opened the door of the Church to the civil servants, fervently commending himself to God, Blessed Mary, and the patron saints of his Church. He died for the law of God and the freedom of the Church and won the glorious palm of martyrdom. This story is taken from the *Annals of the Church of England* written by Arfold.

One can almost immediately recognize the similarities between the actions of the National Assembly and the deeds of Henry II. Through the decrees, the National Assembly has taken upon herself tasks that belong to the spiritual authority. She has forced all clerics to take an oath of loyalty, beginning with the bishops and then the other ecclesiastics. The bishops and others will now take an oath to the Assembly, but the only oath they should make is to the Pope. The Assembly has stolen the goods of the Church, just as Henry II did. Of course, Thomas demanded their restitution. The most Christian King of France has been coerced to assent to these decrees. Finally, the bishops of France, like those of England, have proposed to the Assembly an oath that would distinguish between the rights of the temporal authority and those of the spiritual authority. They would submit in purely civil areas. They will not submit in areas over which the Assembly lacks competence. The bishops who have proposed this resemble the generous Christian soldiers who served under Julian the Apostate. Augustine eulogized them in these terms: "Julian was an unfaithful emperor, even an apostate, a detestable idolater. Nevertheless, he had in his army Christian soldiers who faithfully obeyed him. But when it came to the cause of Christ, they only knew he who was in Heaven. If someone commanded them to worship idols and to offer them incense, they would choose God over the Emperor. When he ordered them to go into battle or march against an enemy, they would immediately obey. They distinguished between their Eternal Lord and their temporal lord." Nevertheless, the National Assembly would reject such a distinction, just as Henry II refused to allow the insertion of the clause, *salvo ordine suo*. From the first point to the last, the decrees of the National Assembly are of the same level of wickedness as the deeds of Henry II.

But the National Assembly has not simply limited herself to following in the steps of Henry II. She also imitates Henry VIII who usurped the primacy in the Church of England and entrusted all of its power to Cromwell, who was corrupted by Zwinglianism. He declared him his vicar general with respect to spiritual matters. He gave him the responsibility of visiting all of the monasteries in his realm. Cromwell in turn entrusted this task to Cramner, his friend, who was motivated by the same principles. They were both fixated on one task, stabilizing the ecclesiastical primacy of the King. They wanted the King to be acknowledged as possessing in himself all the power which the Church received from Jesus Christ. The visits were made to the monasteries with the purpose of suppressing them, committing sacrilege and stealing their ecclesiastical goods. The visitors used the occasion to satisfy their cupidity, avarice and hatred of the Pope. Henry VIII was able to pretend that his oath of loyalty was nothing other than a mere formula for reinforcing the promise of temporal obedience and purely civil fidelity that bishops had made. But the effect was to abolish all the authority of the Holy See. In the same way, the Assembly that currently prevails in France has named its constitution "Civil Constitution of the Clergy." In reality, the decrees subvert all ecclesiastical authority and reduce the communication of the bishops with us to a mere formality, whereby we give our opinions to what has already been done without our approval. Who is not able to see that what the Assembly really had in mind was something similar to the decrees of the two Kings of England, Henry II and Henry VIII. What has passed for a constitution is really nothing more than an almost perfect imitation of the principles of conduct of these two princes. If one can point to any difference, it is only that the modern version is worse than its precursors.

Now that we have compared the two Henrys to each other and their deeds to the actions of the National Assembly, let us proceed to compare the deeds of the Bishop of Autun to those of his colleagues. In order not to dwell on the details too much, it will be sufficient to inspect the decrees of the Civil Constitution of the Clergy, to which he has sworn unwavering loyalty. This will enable us to judge the different reasons behind his belief and the belief of the other members of the episcopacy. The other bishops chose to steadfastly follow the law of God with great courage. They put themselves at the service of the doctrines taught by their predecessors. They remained closely united to the Chair of Peter. They exercised and preserved their rights with daring. They opposed innovations with all of their power. They waited for our response, seeing it as a guide for their conduct. They spoke with one voice. Together they confessed the One Faith. They held to one tradition and discipline. We are shocked to see that the Bishop of Autun is deaf to the reasoning of his colleagues and blind to their example. Bossuet, bishop of Meaux, a very well-known author among you and upon whom no suspicion can be cast, compared Thomas of Canterbury and Thomas Cranmer. The contrast could be very useful for us in this case. We will quote the Bossuet here so that those who read it can judge for themselves the points of similarity between Thomas of Canterbury and Thomas Cranmer and between the Bishop of Autun and his fellow bishops. "Saint Thomas of Canterbury resisted the iniquity of the Kings. Thomas Cranmer prostituted his conscience on their behalf and flattered their passions. One was banished, deprived of his goods, and persecuted spiritually and bodily. He was afflicted in every way and achieved the glorious freedom of speaking the Truth. In doing all this, he courageously showed a healthy detachment from this life and all of the goods associated with it. The other, in order to please his prince, spent his life making shameful dissimulations. He never stopped acting against his conscience. Canterbury struggled to the death to defend the smallest rights of the Church. He defended the prerogatives that Jesus Christ won for us by his Blood, prerogatives that pious Kings have always recognized. Cranmer freed the Kings of the earth from the deposit of sacred tradition, the Word of God, divine worship, the Sacraments, the Keys of Peter, the exercise of legitimate authority, censures: in short, the very Faith itself. By doing this, he put the important parts of faith under the yoke of temporal power. He arrogated all ecclesiastical power to the royal throne. When this happened, the Church had no more power than what the world granted to it in any given moment. Canterbury always remained fearless and pious during his life. He showed the most courage in his final hour. Cranmer, always weak and trembling in fear before his master, showed it more than ever as death approached. At 62 years of age and for the rest of his miserable life, he shed his faith and his conscience. It is fitting that this man's name is remembered with fear among men. It is also not easy to excuse his comrades, as one would have to invent many rationalizations. The facts do not lie. The glory of Saint Thomas of Canterbury, however, will always live on in the Church. France and England will both remember his virtues with reverence. They will not be forgotten."

More surprising still, the Bishop of Autun does not seem to have been affected by the declaration made by the chapter of his Cathedral church, 1 December 1790. He should blush with shame. because he is given good example by the very ones to whom he should give good example, whom he should instruct, and whom he should illuminate with good doctrine. In this declaration, the priests of Autun, helped by the true principles that the Church has articulated, rose up against the errors in the Constitution of the Clergy. They expressed themselves in the following terms: "The chapter of Autun declares: (1) that it will formally adhere to the exposition of principles guiding the creation of the Constitution of the Clergy, an exposition written by the bishops acting as representatives to the National Assembly on 30 October. (2) that this constitution would require us to abandon our conscience; therefore, we cannot participate directly or indirectly in carrying out the plan of the new Constitution of the Clergy: especially where it concerns the suppression of the Cathedral church. As a consequence, this chapter will continue its sacred and canonical tasks, including caring for the numerous institutions attached to the Church, until it is forced into a position in which it is impossible to carry them out. (3) that In its role as protector of the goods and the rights of the bishop, and by virtue of the spiritual jurisdiction that is given to Cathedral churches, the chapter cannot consent to the temporal authority redrawing the boundaries of the diocese of Autun, while the office of the bishop is empty."

We do not wish to let the Bishop of Autun, or those who may have made the mistake of following his example of perjury, forget what the Church pronounced concerning the bishops who attended the Council of Rimini. They fell for the ambiguous and cunning traps laid for them by the Arians as well as the fear provoked by the menaces of the Emperor Constance. They signed a formula designed by the Arians to fool them. Pope Liberius warned them that, if they persisted in their error, "he would vigorously apply the spiritual punishments of the Catholic Church against them." Saint Hilary of Poitiers expelled the bishop Saturnin from the Cathedral of Arles. Saturnin had obstinately persisted in holding on to the opinions of the Arian bishops. Saint Damasus further confirmed the judgment of Pope Liberius. He published a synodal letter in a council along with ninety other bishops. This letter stipulated that Eastern Bishops should publically retract their errors if they wished to remain Catholic. He understood that there were some who "thought that their weakness prevented them from taking steps to return to communion with us. We take away from these the title of bishop, so that the people can be freed from error and breathe easily once again." It is difficult to deny that the Bishop of Autun and his followers do realize that they are in a similar position to the bishops whom Liberius, Hilary and Damasus corrected. They know what to expect if they fail to retract their oaths.

We have not naively examined and set forth these points according to arbitrary, personal criteria. Instead, we have tested them against the sure standard of sacred doctrine. We now turn to you, our dear brothers, for whom we have the most heart-felt concern. You are our joy and our crown jewels. We know that you surely do not need to be encouraged by exhortations, since we are honored to boast in the glory of the courageous faith that you have made shine forth in the midst of sufferings, disgraces, and persecutions. You have published for your flocks excellent works to explain your refusal to take the Oath of Loyalty to the Civil Constitution of the Clergy. Your arguments are well-grounded. Nevertheless, because we live in a time in which the circumstances are calamitous, those who wish to stand with the Lord must diligently guard against all dangers. Therefore, not through our own merits, but by virtue of our responsibilities as pastor of the flock, we urge you to do everything that is in your power to preserve the concord that exists among you. We wish you to remain united with one heart in principles and in deeds. You will be able to repel with one spirit any insidious traps that the National Assembly might set. With the help of God, you will defend the Catholic religion against their endeavors. Nothing will help your enemies succeed more than if division arises among yourselves. A perfect concord, an unalterable union of thought and will remain the strongest ramparts and the best weapons to oppose the efforts and the plots of the enemy. We recall here the words that our predecessor Saint Pius V used to encourage the chapter and canons of Besançon who found themselves in similar circumstances as yours: "May your souls remain strong and constant. Do not let dangers or threats weaken your resolve." Remember the fearlessness of David before the giant, the courage of the Maccabees before Antiochus. Recall how Basil resisted Valens, how Hilary opposed Constance, how Yves of Chartes stood up to King Philippe. We have already arranged for public prayers to be said for those who share our concerns. We have urged the King to refuse his assent to the decrees. We have counseled two archbishops about their duty to give the King good advice. Furthermore, We have noticed that the Third Estate is currently violently disposed. In order to calm them down, inasmuch as we have the power to do so, for the moment we have ceased demanding the taxes that France owes to the Apostolic Chamber. The rights to these funds derive from ancient covenants that have been confirmed through many years' usage. This sacrifice on our part has not been recognized as it ought to have been. In addition, we are sorry to see that some members of the National Assembly have instigated, fostered, and carried out the fire of revolt in Avignon. Against them, we will not cease to invoke the rights of the Holy See. Until now, we have not had recourse to the spiritual punishments that the Church could use against the authors of this unfortunate Civil Constitution of the Clergy. We have opposed all of the outrages with mildness and patience. We have done everything on our part prevent France from falling into schism. We have encouraged peace within your nation. Even now, animated by the counsels of paternal charity that are outlined at the end of your exposition, we ask that you let us know if there is anything that we might do to help bring about a reconciliation among all those involved in these affairs. The great distances between places prevent us from determining what means would be best for this task. But placed as you are in the center of events, perhaps you will discover some means that neither harm Catholic doctrine in any way nor weaken the universal discipline of the Church. If you discover some such means, we ask that you let us know, so that we might study the proposal and submit it to mature deliberations. It remains for us to beseech Our Lord to keep such wise and vigilant pastors in his Church for a long time. Along with these prayers we give to you our apostolic blessing, dear sons and venerable brothers, from the bottom of our heart, and as a product of our paternal affection.

Given in Rome, at Saint Peter, 10 March 1791, the sixteenth year of our pontificate.

To our very dear son in Jesus Christ, his very Christian Majesty, Louis XVI, King of France
Pope Pius VI

Health and apostolic blessing to our very dear son in Jesus Christ.

If we have deferred responding to the last letter of Your Majesty until now, we hope that you will excuse this delay in order to consider the motives that have held us back. You will recognize the first motive immediately. Given the haste with which you gave your sanction to carry out the decrees of the Civil Constitution of the Clergy, our response could not reach you in time. We were about to send you our response when your courier arrived. We were then informed that the very actions about which you had consulted us had already been carried out. This then is what caused our delay, or rather it imposed an obligation on us. We sensed the need to demonstrate how the articles of this constitution are in opposition to Catholic doctrine and are unable to be reconciled with its principles. This deep-seated opposition prevents us from ever being able to approve these articles, even provisionally or even for a minimum amount of time.

We undertook to show this truth clearly. We had to find time to carry this out while also attending to the innumerable other matters that continually occupy us. With all the affairs that have delayed us, it has not aggrieved us to see that the teachings of the bishops did not need our instruction first. At the same time, the majority of the members of the National Assembly, who authored that fatal constitution, attributed to us alone a doctrine that the bishops also opposed in a flurry of pastoral letters, warnings, and edicts. The bishops identified the calumnies of the modern philosophers and enemies of our legitimate jurisdiction and stopped them at the source. These "legislators" have reported that these teachings come from us alone, when in fact they also come from a great number of pious and wise bishops who were expressing their own ideas. The refractories must admit that the bishops have done nothing more than to manifest their obedience to true principles.

There is no doubt that the bishops have fought for a good cause. We have studied with diligent attention the constitution against which they have acted. From this study it became clear that, if one took the so-called Civil Oath, one could not escape the charge of heresy. In taking the Oath, a person gives support to a constitution that is nothing more than a bundle of heresies. Your Majesty will be able to see this once you read our response to the bishops of France. A copy accompanies this letter. Your Majesty is committed, by a promise put in our hands, to live and die in the bosom of the Catholic faith. This promise is a powerful consolation for us. Surely, you know that for you, however, this will be the cause of continual and bitter sorrow, because by sanctioning the constitution, you have torn the unity of the Catholic faith, especially for all of those who, out of weakness, will take the Oath or intellectually assent to the erroneous principles that guided the creation of the Civil Constitution of the Clergy. In this way you have renounced all of the honor and the glory that you would have won had you risen to defend religion before your Estates. Instead, by this act performed out of weakness, you have departed from the company of your ancestors who supported religion in their times with zeal and daring.

We cannot prevent ourselves from placing before you the example of Saint Avitus, bishop of Vienna. It is as stark a contrast as we can offer. This saint, who lived at the beginning of the sixth century, addressed the King of the Burgundians, Gondebauld, at the Council of Epaone (today Paunas in Dauphine or Jenne in Savoie, on the Rhone) with these words full of evangelical freedom: "Tumultuous circumstances should not become a reason for you to dispense from giving public witness to the Creator of the universe. This is an essential point of religion. Even in the middle of popular frenzies, it is necessary to make a public confession of the faith that you simultaneously affirm at the bottom of your heart with a clear voice.

To this consideration, you ought to add the memory of the promises that you made to God on 11 July 1775, the day of your coronation. At that time, you promised to defend and preserve the rights of the Church and the privileges of the episcopacy in their integrity. You did this by a solemn oath, an oath which you should see is in absolute opposition to the Oath that is required by these most recent decrees. The one goal of these most recent decrees is to obliterate all the rights of the Church, to make the bishops leave their sees, and to chase them from their dioceses.

Indeed, we wish there to be, and we know that there are, laws of government that belong entirely to the civil power and that are thoroughly distinct from the laws of the Church. We affirm obedience to civil laws. At the same time, we demand that lay powers not violate spiritual laws which remain uniquely under our authority. A majority of the bishops have already made an exposition of this doctrine to us. They have declared their intention to take an oath of loyalty with respect to everything that pertains to the secular authority. At the same time, they have formally declined to take an oath of loyalty to the secular authority that pertains to the rights of the spiritual power. It is of great importance that Your Majesty examines very closely the current circumstances in your realm. Your kingdom has fallen into a deplorable condition. The revolution has subverted the foundations of the religion established by our Redeemer. Recklessness and madness, brought about by unrestrained passions, have broken out everywhere. Man has exiled God and put himself in his place. He has forged new doctrines, a new hierarchy, and a new discipline. He has freed men to follow whatever violence their wills conceive of. He suppresses the True Religion, which until this time was predominant and most esteemed. Now, he openly preaches and praises the "complete liberty" of Man. But France, where these so-called freedoms are expressed, fails to leave her citizens free to exercise the dictates of their conscience.

Thus stands the condition of things. Any good Catholic or sane political man should be able to recognize this. It is necessary that Your Majesty look into himself and see the true norms that inform his conscience. He should maturely reflect on them. He should also consider the counsel that his good and wise bishops provide him to help him discern what is best. He should do everything in his power not to leave the bishops without a patron, and, at the very least, to ensure that the body of priests not be prohibited from continuing the religion of their fathers. You will easily understand when you read our letter to the bishops of France that we have the right to use our authority to oppose the clear errors of the revolutionaries. But, we have instead chosen to act in a way that is lenient. That was our plan of conduct and it will continue to be our way of proceeding. We understand that men in this age have been seduced and led astray. Inasmuch as our ministry allows it, we will hope to lead them gently back to the bosom of the Church. We have also asked the bishops to propose concrete suggestions that we can submit to rational examination (if any such ways exist at this moment). We will see if they are applicable in these circumstances. We have also asked them to let us know how we can help them administer the needs of their dioceses.

One of the principal censures that we levied against the Bishop of Autun consists of the grave scandal that he has caused throughout the Catholic world by taking the Civil Oath of Loyalty. We understand that a few other bishops have done so along with him. We are certain that among the others is Cardinal de Loménie who has made himself known to us through several error-filled letters fraught with his poorly founded political sensibilities. We have given him our response, and we include a copy along with this letter. It seems that two other Cardinals have behaved in the same manner as the Bishop of Autun and followed his example. Your Majesty should not be surprised to learn that we will carry out the responsibilities of our office. If they do not retract their oaths, we will act against them. We will do what our predecessors have done in similar cases.

Your Majesty should not fail to distinguish the essential differences between ecclesiastical and temporal government, the opinion of Saint Avitus, and the oath that you took on the day of your coronation. You will not find a contradiction between the duties imposed on you as a very Christian King and as the eldest son of the Church. You will merit the approval of the Universal Church, the Holy See, and the help of the King of Kings.

These are the paternal sentiments that fill our heart for Your Majesty and for your august family. Receive our apostolic blessing which we give to you from the bottom of our heart.

Given in Rome, at Saint Peter, 10 March 1791, the seventeenth year of our pontificate.

To our dear son John Guegan, rector of Pontivy, in Paris
Pope Pius VI

Health and apostolic blessing to our dear son.

We are responding to the letter, dear son, that you wrote to us on the 12th of this month. We are giving you the response that you eagerly awaited from the Holy See, the source of any legitimate ministry in the ecclesiastical order. You have asked us what you should do if your fellow citizens are unhappy that you do not wish to be the bishop of Vannes. They have persisted in their efforts to obtain your consent, which until this point you have refused. It is your right to act this way.

The response follows. The canonical reasons that have led you to voluntarily refuse the position offered to you are worthy of praise. They are more than sufficient and have rightly persuaded you. You should not alter your resolve. Nor should you let any alternative suggestions, contentions, threats or persecution lead you to change. Persecution, if it should come, will only give you greater glory. There is nothing greater that a Catholic man, an ecclesiastic, or a parish priest can endure and suffer for the cause of God.

You have expressly declared that you lack the audacity to take the chair of a bishop who was still living. Such a man still merits and receives your respect. You know – and admitted as much in your letter – that he never resigned his position. You will not consent in any way to the decrees of the National Assembly, decrees that are contrary to the holy canons and to justice. They are schismatic, and they are essentially no laws at all. There is nothing that the canons detest more greatly, nor which they defend with more rigorous punishments, than to take a pastor of the Church and give his office to someone else, to consecrate another bishop in his place, with the same title, and to invade his church. This is a schismatic act and an attempt at sacrilege.

We believe that it is our task not only to encourage you, but also to seriously warn you, that you should persevere in your first resolution not to allow any bishop to impose his hands on you. No one, no archbishop, no bishop, can demand this of you nor grant it to you without being culpable of a most horrible crime. The Church has not lost its legitimate pastor. There has not been a canonical election. Our apostolic approval has not been granted. All these things are lacking. All of them are necessary in order for a legitimate canonical mission to occur. If an ordination is done in any other way, the one who is ordained lacks all legitimate power and jurisdictional authority – not to mention that he has committed a great sacrilege. Any acts that he carries out are null and are devoid of validity.

There is a serious defect here that is a consequence of the nature of these things. This cannot be covered up or minimized. There is no obstacle to such decrees in the case of someone who accepts the government of a church with the intention of turning it over to the legitimate pastor as soon as possible. A will that acts by way of invasion destroys its validity. Laws passed in another way by an illegitimate and secular power with the purpose of replacing the laws of the Church are not to be followed. Their purpose is to divide and distribute tasks which belong to the dignity of the episcopal office.

A pastor chased from his office by violence and injustice still keeps his jurisdiction and his responsibility of caring for his flock while he is suffering in these conditions. We are not able to permit another person to be ordained for a church that has its bishop. Nor can we ordain a coadjutor bishop. This is the custom of the Holy See. We only grant coadjutors in the circumstances outlined in the canons. The case we have here is one in which we see the violent subversion of the most sacred rights. In addition, the bishop has to consent to receive a coadjutor. Ordinarily, we ask him and we wait for his consent before granting one.

There is nothing more for you to do now, save to resist their efforts using your ingenuity, eloquence, and industry, and to convince your fellow citizens to remain loyal to their legitimate bishop. They should give no support to another bishop who attempts to invade the church of their legitimate bishop.

We declare to you once again that you have rightly consulted us to avoid any schismatic actions. Be certain of this, if you renounce the approval and praise of good men, which up to this point you have received, and if you consent to your election as bishop against our will and our warnings, then you would be in open schism. Those who have already committed similar elections are already in schism, and we are unable to express in words our sorrow at this fact. The bishops who have dared to impose their hands on them have also committed sacrilege.

We have experienced a real joy seeing in you sentiments that are rightly opposed to the usurpers. We are certain that you will not cede in any essential matter. You will do as our beloved son Thomas des Vauspons, vicar-general of Dole, has done. While there is no episcopal office in Laval, he was elected bishop of that city. He wrote to us asking what he should do. But, spurred on by his conscience he rejected the office that the Assembly offered him even before he received a response from us, a response that resembles the one which we sent to you. The bishop of Rennes has used him as an example to Le Coz, the director of the college at Quimper, who, in ambiguous terms, shared his notions about his election as bishop of L'Ille and Vilaine. You can see the beautiful response of the Bishop of Rennes dated the 7 of this month, which we have copied.

Finally, with respect to the election and consecration of bishops in those churches that still have pastors or that lack pastors, you will find this amply treated in the letter that we wrote to our venerable brothers, the archbishops and bishops of France, dated 10 March and sent out the next day by an extraordinary courier. Copies should have been published by now in France. There you should find the guidelines for your conduct and what you should do next. In the meantime, we praise your enthusiasm for religion and your affection for us in the Lord. We grant you our apostolic blessing with all of our heart.

Sent from Rome, 30 March 1791, the seventeenth year of our pontificate.

Letter to the Archbishops of France, and a commendatory letter, concerning the Civil Oath that has been set for ecclesiastics and the election and consecration of pseudo-bishops, and to the Cardinals, archbishops, bishops, chapters, clergy and people of the realm of France.
Pope Pius VI

Venerable brother: may God grant you health and our apostolic blessing.

The evil perturbations that agitate the kingdom of France become more serious as each day passes. In order to fulfill our apostolic responsibilities, we are forced to follow our letter of 10 March with an address to our dear sons, the chapters, the clergy, and the people of France. We must warn them of the schism that is being introduced and established within the country. This is why we have made as quickly as possible new copies of our letter and circulated them by hand. We wanted to send proof of our confidence in their deeds to the metropolitans. We have good reason for our confidence in them and in the bishops of each province. We have resolved to send several copies to each metropolitan, so that they in turn, can communicate to the bishops, the clergy, and the people of their province. That way, they can all direct their struggles, voices, and efforts toward the same goal. With this in mind, we have sent you , our venerable brother, a certain number of copies of this letter, persuaded that your pastoral concern will respond perfectly to our commitment. We also give you and the flock that is entrusted to your care our apostolic blessing, with the most tender affection.

Given at Rome, from Saint Peter, under the seal of the fisherman, 13 April 1791, the seventheenth year of our pontificate.

To our beloved sons the Cardinals of the Holy Roman Church, to our venerable brother archbishops, bishops, and our sons the chapters, clergy and people of the kingdom of France.
Pope Pius VI

Beloved sons, venerable brothers: health and our apostolic blessings on you.

Charity, as Saint Paul teaches us, is patient and kind. It suffers and bears all things, even as it waits in hope to end by a spirit of meekness the errors that have begun to overtake the minds and hearts of men. Indeed, error makes greater progress in our own days, and many people have fallen into schism. Even now the laws of charity guide us. These laws are inseparable from the other duties that we are called to carry out by our apostolic ministry despite our unworthiness. They demand that we be paternal but at the same time prompt and efficacious in applying the medicine to the disease that is sprouting forth, in making clear the horror of the errors for which these men are responsible, and in making known the serious nature of the canonical punishments which they have incurred. As a result, those who have lost the way of Truth may see their errors, abandon them, and return to the Church. She awaits their return as a good mother, with her arms open and ready to receive them. At the same time, the rest of the mature faithful will be able to avoid the fraud perpetrated by pseudo-pastors who have gained authority over the sheepfold by a way other than the legitimate door. They can only seek to ravish, devour, and destroy the flock.

We hold before our eyes these divine precepts. We have just heard the rumors of war which the modern philosophers, gathered together and constituting a majority in the National Assembly of France, have declared against the Catholic faith. We have cried bitter tears before God. We have shared our anxiety with the Cardinals of the Holy Roman Church. We have also ordered public and private prayers to be said for this intention. We have already encouraged our son in Christ, Louis, the very Christian King of France, by a letter dated 9 July 1790, not to give his sanction to the Civil Constitution of the Clergy. That would entail leading his nation into error and opening up a schism within his realm.

We explained that it would be absolutely impossible for a purely political assembly to claim for itself the right to change the universal discipline of the Church, to overturn the authority of the Fathers and the decrees of Councils, to reverse the order of the hierarchy, to arbitrarily regulate the election of bishops, to suppress episcopal sees, and to replace ancient and respectable forms long established in the Church with new and vicious ones.

To instill these exhortations more deeply in the soul of your very Christian King, on the 10th of the same month, we wrote two letters in the form of briefs to our venerable brothers, the archbishops of Bordeaux and Vienne. We encouraged them to act as personal assistants to the King. We encouraged them to unite their efforts with our own, that is, to attempt to prevent the royal sanction. They could thereby help prevent giving any aid to this constitution. If not, the realm would sooner or later fall prey to a schism. The newly elected bishops, following the new forms, would themselves become schismatics. We would find ourselves obliged to declare them intruders and deprive them of all ecclesiastical jurisdiction. With a view to clearly proving our solicitude had for its sole object the good of religion, we have ceased requesting the payments which were owed to the apostolic chamber, according to ancient treaties and continuous custom.

We are certain that the King could never of his own accord have given assent to this constitution. But, pushed by the National Assembly he at last succumbed to the pressure and added his authority to the constitution. In his letters of 28 July, 6 September, and 16 December he asked us if he could approve, first five, then, seven articles, at least provisionally. In their substance, these articles were no more than abridged versions of the new constitution.

We clearly saw that it would be impossible for us to give our approval or to tolerate any of these decrees without opposing established canonical norms. At the same time, we did not want to give our enemies the opportunity to seize this occasion to further deceive the people. They could do this by popularizing the rumor that we were opposed to all forms of reconciliation. We hope to always follow the path of kindness and patience, and so we made clear to the King, by our letter of 17 August, that we would carefully examine the articles. In addition, we would gather together a council of Cardinals, and, once gathered, together we would record our considered reflections on each of the articles. We assembled twice, 24 September and 16 December. We gave serious reflection to the five and the seven proposed articles. A unanimous opinion prevailed, that we should first ask the bishops of France their opinion about these articles. We also wished to know if there might be a canonical solution, seeing that our distance from the place might not permit us to see one. We had asked the King for the same opinion.

We were greatly afflicted by events, but our sorrows were lightened when we learned that the majority of bishops in France, moved by their devotion to their pastoral responsibilities, and inflamed by a love for Truth, took their own initiative to oppose this constitution. They resisted it in all of those matters in which it touched on the government of the Church. Our beloved son, the Cardinal of Rochefoucault, our venerable brothers the Archbishops of Aix and other archbishops, and thirty bishops all provided us with newfound reasons for consolation. When they sent us the exposition of their opinions on the principles of the Civil Constitution of the Clergy, they asked for our counsel in this critical set of circumstances. They had recourse to us as a teacher and as a father. They wished to know the norms of conduct that should govern their own. This greatly increased our consolation. Many bishops, united with their leaders, embraced this exposition of principles. Among the thirty one bishops in the realm, there were but four dissidents. To this vast majority of bishops, one could add a number of chapters, a multitude of clergy, and parish priests. With one unanimous mind the entire Gallican Church embraced the same doctrine.

Without any undue delay, we began to work and to closely examine every article of the constitution. But, the National Assembly of France acted as though they had never heard the united voice of the Church. They were so far from turning back from the enterprise they had started, that the constancy of the bishops only further irritated them. They clearly saw, and there could be no doubt here, that they were not going to find among the metropolitans and the bishops anyone who would force himself to believe that he had the power to consecrate bishops whom laymen, heretics, infidels, and Jews had elected in various municipal districts, as the published decrees demanded. They were convinced that this absurd form of ecclesiastical government could not continue to exist. Without bishops, all appearances of having a church evaporate. So, they thought of more absurd addenda, 15 and 27 November, and then 2, 4, and 25 January 1791. By these decrees, also submitted for the royal assent, it was ordained that, if the metropolitan or the eldest bishop refused to consecrate the newly elected bishops, they would be moved to another department. By this means, they could with one blow deprive the Church in France of all the bishops and clergy that had proven to be loyal to the Catholic faith. They have ordered all of the clergy of the first and second orders to take the Oath of Loyalty with no exception. They must conform to all of the rules relative to the articles of the constitution, as well as any that might be established in the future. They have also declared that those who refuse to take the Oath are to be deprived of their ecclesiastical functions. They will consider their parishes and their episcopal offices vacated. The legitimate pastors will be chased from their offices by force. The municipal districts will then proceed with elections for new bishops and new parish priests. These newly elected clergy will not be accountable to metropolitans or to bishops. Instead, they will answer to the directory. The Assembly will nominate a bishop for this position. He will confirm elections and provide their institution.

The sorrow that we felt upon hearing of these final decrees completely disheartened us. They magnified our task. They increased the number of concerns we had to address in our response to the bishops. Because of all of our concerns, we asked for more public prayers to be said in order to beseech the Father of Mercies to grant us mercy. These decrees moved the bishops of France to further action. They had already published excellent responses against the Civil Constitution of the Clergy. Now, they have published new pastoral letters for their flocks. They have struggled with every ounce of their being against the Oath of Loyalty, against the efforts of the Assembly to get rid of bishops along with the efforts to place new bishops in empty offices, and against the election and institution of new pastors. The result: the entire Gallican Church is confessing and unanimously agreesthat taking the Civil Oath would constitute perjury, that it would be a sacrilege, a deed unworthy of a Catholic man. If anyone took the Oath, his subsequent actions were schismatic, in vain, and liable to the most serious punishments.

The Gallican clergy held to their claims by their deeds. They deserve high praise for this. Almost all the bishops and a great majority of clergy refused to take the Oath. They showed an unconquerable strength of spirit in doing so. Fittingly, the enemies of religion acknowledged that all of their plans were in vain, unless they could find a way to subjugate an ambitious or weak-minded bishop. Those who preached the Oath in support of the constitution and imposed their sacrilegious hands on new bishops were so few that almost none were led into schism. Among the leaders of those conquered by deception and fraud, Charles the bishop of Autun stands at the head. He is the most ardent supporter of the constitution. The second is Jean-Joseph, bishop of Lydda. The third is Louis, bishop of Orléans. The fourth is Charles, bishop of Viviers, and the fifth, Cardinal de Loménie, archbishop of Sens. Several unfortunate priests of the second order – their numbers small – followed the lead of these bishops.

With regard to Cardinal de Loménie, he wrote a letter to us on 25 November 1790. He rationalized taking the Oath by stating that he did not grant his interior assent to its propositions. He saw that it was quite unclear whether he should refuse laying his hands on the elected bishops or not (up to that point he had held back). Persuaded that it made a difference that none of the bishops assented to the consecration of the elected bishops, and that he had increased the possibility of schism, we judged it appropriate to interrupt our response to the bishops, which was almost done, and to write to the Cardinal without delay on 23 February. We showed him the errors in his reasons for taking the Oath as well as the punishment that the canons imposed upon him. We also indicated that, though it would bring great melancholy to our soul, we would be forced to remove him from his position as Cardinal. He could avoid this step if he were to repair the public scandal that he had caused by retracting his deeds in a satisfactory way. We addressed the doubt that he had expressed on the consecration of irregularly elected bishops. We encouraged him to stay away from these deeds and that he should not under any pretext participate in instituting new bishops. To do so would be to allow refractory priests into the bosom of the Church. What he was trying to do was something that belongs only to the authority of the Holy See, as indicated in the decisions of the Council of Trent. If any bishop or metropolitan dared to take upon himself this power, we would be obliged by the duties of our office to declare schismatic both those who were instituted and those who attempted the institution. Any act that either of them committed after this would be considered null.

Once we fulfilled the obligations of the office of supreme pastor as reason commanded, we returned to writing our response to the bishops. It seemed that, each day, new dimensions arose in this project, which had become long and laborious. Finally, with the help of Heaven, we had the strength to complete it. We again reviewed all of the articles of the new Constitution of the Clergy so that nothing would escape our notice. We then pronounced our judgment and that of the Apostolic See, in keeping with what the French bishops had asked. We also realized that the people of France were eager to learn our response. There can be no doubt in the minds of the faithful now that this new Constitution of the Clergy as a whole and in its several parts is founded on heretical principles. It is contrary to Catholic dogma. In some parts it is sacrilegious, schismatic, and destroys the right of primacy of the Holy See and of the Church. It is contrary to both the ancient and modern discipline of the Church. It could not have been devised according to any other plan than made for the destruction of the Catholic religion. Under this Constitution all other religions are given freedom. It removes legitimate Catholic pastors and takes away the goods of the Church, but grants full liberty to men who lead other sects and allows them to rest easy in the possession of all their goods.

We have until now clearly demonstrated all of these things, while at the same time remaining as kind as possible in our approach to these matters. We could declare the authors of all of the evil acts of the Civil Constitution of the Clergy to be cut off from the Church. But, before taking such action, we must repeat our basic position. They should renounce their errors, which we have made clear in the way that the Holy See has always prescribed in these cases. If they do not, we will be compelled to declare all of them schismatic. This includes the authors of the Constitution, those who have taken the Oath, those who have been established as new pastors, those who have consecrated new bishops, and those newly consecrated bishops. All of these, whoever they are, lack a legitimate mandate and communion with the Church.

We have now seconded the inclinations of the French nation, inasmuch as we have shown them to be without prejudice towards dogma and the universal discipline of the Church. Following the opinion of the Cardinals whom we assembled to study this matter, we have repeated to the bishops what we had previously written to the very Christian King. We have encouraged those who find themselves in the midst of the actual events to propose a reasonable course of action to us, if one can be found – one that harms neither Catholic dogma nor universal discipline. We will deliberate and examine any suggestions they send. We have given our sense of the matter to the very Christian King and we have also sent him a copy of our response to the bishops. We have encouraged him in the Lord, so that he might gather around himself the wiser bishops. Together they might find the medicine that would best heal the wound. Perhaps it would come from the exercise of royal authority. We have also made clear to him that we will act in accord with the pastoral responsibilities of our office in keeping with what our predecessors have done, when faced with those who obstinately persist in their errors.

We sent our two letters to the King and to the bishops, dated 10 March, the following day by extraordinary courier. In the meantime, an extraordinary courier came from France on the 15. He informed us that on 24 February the Bishop of Autun carried out a schismatic act. He had already been infected by the crime of perjury. He was already guilty of defection. He had abandoned the Church from which he exercised his legitimate authority and handed it over to the temporal power. Instead of following the good example of his chapter, he allied himself with the bishop of Babylone and Lydda. We honored the former with the pallium and subsidized him with a pension for life. He has shown himself to be the worthy successor of another bishop of Babylone, Dominique Varlet, well known for his participation in the schism of the Church of Utrecht. The latter, guilty of perjury, has fallen into a condition in which he deserves hatred and indignation from good men. He is in this status because he has dissented from the right doctrine of the bishop and head of the Church of Basle, of which he is a suffragan. On this day (the 24), these two bishops, cooperating with the Bishop of Autun, dared to impose their sacrilegious hands on Louis-Alexandre Expilly and Claude-Eustache-François Marolles in the Church of the Priests of the Oratory.

They did so without receiving any mandate from the Holy See. They also failed to make the required oath of obedience to the Sovereign Pontiff. They made neither the examen nor the profession of faith, actions prescribed by the Roman Pontiff and which must be observed throughout the universal Church. They have neglected, violated, and trampled on legitimate laws. One cannot licitly ignore that the first of these bishops has been irregularly installed as the bishop of Quimper against the repeated objections of the chapter of that church. The nomination of the second as bishop of Soissons was even less proper. This church already had a legitimate pastor, our venerable brother Henri-Joseph-Claude de Bourdeilles. He rightly thought that he had been wrongly deprived of his office. He energetically argued against so profoundly disrespectful a deed, and quickly came to the aid of his diocese by publishing his letter the next day, the 25.

It has furthermore been brought to our attention that the supposed bishop of Lydda is guilty of a new crime. On 27 February, he along with two other false bishops, Expilly and Marolles, and in the same church, sacrilegiously consecrated the parish priest Saurine as bishop of Acqs. This Church already had a virtuous pastor, our venerable brother Charles-Auguste Lequien. This action led to Jean-Joseph Gobel, the bishop of Lydda, to be elevated to the See of Paris, which had a living archbishop. They have followed the example of Ischiras. He accused Athanasius and drove him out of his diocese. In order to compensate Ischiras for his crime and remarkable obsequiousness, the false Council of Tyr named him bishop of that city.

This troublesome and sad news cast us into a state of sorrow and confusion. But we rose again with hope in God. On 17 March, we gathered the council of Cardinals once again, so that they might reveal their thoughts on these matters of such serious consequence. And while we were reviewing those things about which we hoped to deliberate with the Cardinals, another courier from France arrived on the 21. He informed us that the bishop of Lydda, who seemed to grow more wicked with every action, had allied himself with the pseudo-bishops Expilly and Saurine. On 6 March, in the same church as before and with the same sacrilegious hands, he consecrated the parish priest Massieu, a deputy of the National Assembly, as the bishop of Beauvais. In addition, he consecrated the parish priest Lindet, also a deputy, as the bishop of Evreux, the priest Laurent as bishop of Moulins, and the priest Heraudin as Bishop of Chateauroux. The fact that the first two dioceses already had their legitimate pastors had no effect on his decision to carry out these actions. Two other so-called dioceses had not been erected into episcopal sees by legitimate apostolic authority. Many centuries ago, Saint Leo energetically declared what kind of judgment ought to be passed on those who let themselves be named and consecrated bishops of dioceses that already had bishops to rule and administer them. In a letter addressed to Julian, bishop of Coos, he wrote concerning the case of a certain Theodosius. This man had usurped the office of the living bishop, Juvenal. "We should characterize that the man who by stealth takes the place of a living bishop as a subversive. The nature of the deed cannot be doubted. The enemies of the Faith love him."

The Church has always opposed bishops being elected through the turmoil and convulsions of lay assemblies – and with good reason. Usually, the elected is attached to the false opinions of his electors. If you seek a demonstration of this reality, it would suffice to review the pastoral letter that the false bishop Expilly published 25 February. The same courier brought this letter to us. It can have no other purpose than to tear the seamless garment of Christ in two. First he recalls the Oath, better said the perjury, by which he is bound. Then he embraces every article of the Gallican constitution, which he cites almost word for word. He adheres to every opinion expressed in the National Assembly. He claims that the constitution respects all the dogmas of the Church and that it puts the discipline of the Church into a better form. It recalls the purity of the first centuries of Christianity, above all in those parts in which it enables the people to remove clergy. It also re-establishes the rights of metropolitans to institute and consecrate bishops. The author of this letter only repeated in it the first decrees of the National Assembly. To make his point felt more strongly by less skilled readers, he relates our letter of 18 November 1790, as if he actually had communion with the Apostolic See. Addressing his words to each of the orders within his diocese, he exhorts them. He warns all of them that they should receive him as their legitimate pastor and freely embrace the constitution.

What miserable behavior! He pretends to have consulted with us about those things that pertain to the civil government. What daring he has, to take up a defense of the constitution that oversees all ecclesiastical matters! He passes over the fact that almost all of the bishops of France and a host of other ecclesiastics have condemned it and refuted it as contrary to right dogma and destructive of common discipline, above all in the manner of electing and consecrating bishops. It is impossible to miss this truth which is clear at first glance through the document. He cannot dissimulate or cover it up. He can only try to pass over in silence and by design the most absurd decrees that the Assembly has put in the place. Among the other wicked deeds that it carries out, the right of instituting and confirming bishops is placed in the hands of the arbitrary will of the directory.

We hope that this unfortunate man, who has made such great progress on the road to perdition, will read our response to the bishops of France. There we have refuted the monstrous errors to be found in his letters. There he will easily discover the Truth, which he hates, shining brightly in each paragraph. He will be able to judge himself for himself. He will see the truth in the ancient discipline established by the canons of the Council of Nicaea, which he himself has cited. Those canons show that the elected bishop does not obtain a legitimate title from a metropolitan, unless the metropolitan first obtains the rights from the Apostolic see. How is it possible that the bishop Expilly could think that he had a legitimate and canonical mission? The bishop of Quimper depends on the archbishop of Tours. But the archbishop of Tours was not at his institution. Other bishops granted his institution. These bishops belonged to other provinces. If these bishops had the audacity to perform a sacrilegious ordination, they failed even to do it in the proper jurisdiction. They wholly abandoned every aspect of ancient discipline, which they had claimed to follow at least in part. But the practice of recent centuries, several Councils, and concordats have established a modern discipline for granting the power of jurisdiction. According to this discipline, metropolitans have no such power. Instead, the power has returned to the source whence it originated, the Apostolic See. Today, the Roman Pontiff, because of the duties of his office, establishes pastors in the various churches. The Council of Trent describes this (sess. 24, cap. 1, *De Reform.*). Throughout the Catholic Church, there is not a legitimate episcopal consecration unless there is a mandate from the Apostolic See.

In reality, the letters which he gave us were not to help him. It would be better to say that they are evidence to convict him. They show the signs of a schismatic. He sent letters to create the image that he was interested in communion with us. There is no indication that he was hoping to obtain our confirmation. His letters tell of his illegitimate election, as the decrees of the National Assembly ordered him to do. We have followed the example of our predecessors and have refrained from writing directly to him. But we have seriously warned him to advance no further in his actions, and that we hope that he will make progress in returning to us in the future. The bishop of Rennes has given him the same advice. Expilly zealously pressed him to grant his confirmation and institution and the bishop refused to participate. Therefore, the people of his diocese, rather than receiving him, should reject him with horror, as the usurper that he is. We repeat, usurper. He ought to recognize the truth in that word. He has voluntarily rejected it. He began exercising his pastoral duties by committing an unwarranted abuse. He showed his arrogance when, at the end of his first pastoral letter, he dispensed the faithful of the diocese from observing the ecclesial precepts for Lent. "He is a follower of Satan. He has departed from the Truth. He has done evil by falsely presenting himself as having an honor that in reality he lacks, and in having a title which in reality he does not have." Saint Leo the Great wrote these lines describing a similar impostor in a letter that he sent to some bishops in Egypt.

The kingdom of France has historically done important deeds of service for religion. We see that the crimes committed are growing and becoming more serious to the point of establishing a schism. But, we have great affection for France. We see that each day new ministers of the first and second order are elected, that legitimate pastors are thrown out of their offices and driven out of their dioceses, and that rapacious wolves replace them. We are moved to tears when we see such spectacles. And so we must quickly raise up an obstacle to prevent them from sliding further into schism. We will help those in error to return to fulfilling their rightful duties. We will confirm the good in their fine resolutions so that religion will continue to flourish in this kingdom. After receiving the counsel of the Cardinals of the Holy Roman Church, seconding the votes of the entire body of bishops in France, and following the example of our predecessors, by the apostolic power which we have received we order that all Cardinals, archbishops, bishops, abbots, vicars, canons, parish priests, priests, ecclesiastics attached to the military, whether secular or regular, who have taken the Civil Oath – plainly and simply, the Oath which the National Assembly has prescribed, a poisonous spring of numerous errors, the principal cause of the evils that afflict the Church in France – to retract that Oath within forty days of today. Whoever does not retract it will be suspended from exercising Holy Orders. He has fallen into irregularity. He is forbidden to exercise any priestly function.

In particular, we declare the elections of the following, Expilly, Marolles, Saurine, Massieu, Lindet, Laurent, Heraudin, and Gobel to the sees of Quimper, Soissons, Acqs, Beavais, Evreux, Moulins, Chateauroux and Paris to be illegitimate, sacrilegious, and null. We rescind them, erase them and annul them. We do the same to the creation of two new episcopal sees in Moulins and Chateauroux, and any other newly erected sees of this kind.

We declare and we judge that these consecrations were criminal acts. All of them are illicit, illegitimate, sacrilegious, and done against the sanctions contained in the sacred canons. Because these clerics were elected without any right, they lack any ecclesiastical or spiritual jurisdiction over souls. Those who consecrated illicitly are suspended from exercising episcopal powers.

Likewise, we suspend Charles, the bishop of Autun, Jean-Baptiste, the bishop of Babylone, and Jean-Joseph, the bishop of Lydda, from exercising any episcopal powers. They are sacrilegious consecrators or assistants to them. Anyone who helped carry out, worked for, consented to, or gave advice relating to these despicable consecrations are also suspended from performing any priestly function or any other duty that they might exercise.

Therefore, we have strictly forbidden Expilly and anyone else illicitly elected and consecrated from daring to carry out any act of episcopal jurisdiction, under the penalty of suspension,. No authority for the government of souls has been granted to them, or anything that flows from this power. They cannot arrogate it to themselves. They cannot give dimissorial letters for Holy Orders. They cannot establish or institute pastors, vicars, missionaries, functionaries, ministers, or any other function intended to guide souls and administer the Sacraments. Likewise, they can do nothing under the pretext of any necessity to fix, to cut off, or to establish, either conjointly or in the mode of a council, anything relative to ecclesiastical jurisdiction. Any declarations or public edicts, such as dimissorial letters, nominations, or institutions that have been done, are being done, or will be done, along with all of their other outrageous deeds, and all of the effects that follow from them – all of these – lack authority and value.

We likewise place under a similar penalty of suspension those who consecrated and those who were consecrated. They are prohibited from carrying out the Sacrament of Confirmation, from conferring Holy Orders, or exercising in any way the episcopal functions from which they are suspended. We warn those who receive Holy Orders from them, that they also are suspended. If they exercise any functions, they will be liable for irregularity.

In order to prevent the worst evils from happening, we order in the same terms and by the same authority that all other elections made by the electors of the departments or districts, in the form prescribed by the Civil Constitution of the Clergy, for the Cathedral churches or parish priests in France, are illegitimate according to ancient and modern forms, even if the offices are empty. If there is already a bishop in the office, any elections done to replace the bishop are, as always, void, illegitimate, sacrilegious. It unnecessary to expressly declare each one to be so. As a consequence, we break, annul, and abrogate any that took place, are taking place, or will take place. Those elected have no episcopal rights. Anyone elected to be a bishop or parish priest lacks any legitimate ecclesiastical jurisdiction and the spiritual jurisdiction to govern souls. Bishops illicitly consecrated, whom we have already mentioned by name, and any that will be consecrated, are suspended and will be suspended from exercising any ecclesial power. Any priest illegitimately instituted is and will be suspended. We strictly forbid the current or future election of bishops by any metropolitan or any other bishop or that they dare to receive an episcopal consecration from them.

We also prohibit the false bishops and their sacrilegious consecrators, along with all the other archbishops and bishops from undertaking, under any name or pretext that they could devise, from consecrating men who are irregularly elected. We also order all of those who will be named bishops or parish priests to never approach one of these archbishops, bishops, priests, or vicars and to add their name or title to any Cathedral church or parish. Do not attribute any jurisdiction, authority or power to govern souls to them. Any of this would be done under the punishment of suspension and nullity. Only we, or those to whom the apostolic see delegates such authority, have the authority to lift such punishments.

We have used as much leniency as possible when choosing and declaring canonical penalties. Our hope is to lead the evildoers to mend their ways and to prevent the virus from spreading more widely. We have great hope in the Lord that those who have consecrated false bishops, whether the usurpers of Cathedrals or parish churches, and that all the authors and supporters of the Civil Constitution of the Clergy clearly see their error. May they do penance and return to the flock. They have been torn away by intrigue and seduction. For these lost children we have the words of a father. We pray for them. We beseech the Lord for them that they freely remove themselves from their ministry and that they take a step back from the path of perdition upon which they have dared to tread. That path has been cultivated by men immersed in the false philosophy of this century which has spread monstrous teachings among the people, teachings contrary to the teachings of Jesus Christ, the traditions of our Fathers, and the regulations of the Church. But if our mildness and if our paternal warnings do not bear any fruit then let them face the Wrath of God. They should know that we will inflict the severe penalties prescribed by the canons. They should be convinced that we will levy against them anathemas. We will denounce them to the Universal Church as schismatic, cut off from the bosom of the church and from communion with us. It is well said that "if he chooses to lie in the mire of his foolishness, let the decrees remain, and let him have his lot with those whose error he has followed." Saint Leo our predecessor taught this in his letter to Julian the bishop of Coos.

We now directly address you, venerable brothers. With the exception of a small number, you have carried out in an exemplary fashion your pastoral duties. Setting aside human rationalizations, you have openly confessed the Faith. You understood that this would cause you much pain and involve much work. Many dangers have violently come upon you. We praise you as Leo the Great praised the bishops of Egypt who took refuge in Constantinople: "Our heart is filled with compassion at the sufferings that you have endured for upholding the practice of the Catholic Faith. We are well aware of the wounds that you have received from heretics. I have received the news as if I myself bore them. I understand that you have more joy than sorrow, because, strengthened by Our Lord Jesus Christ, you have remained strong and unconquerable in the Gospel and apostolic teaching. The enemies of the Christian faith have estranged you from your churches. You have preferred the injustice of exile, rather than contracting the infection of impiety." It gives us great consolation to learn of your actions. We encourage you to remain strong in your good resolutions. Call to mind the spiritual bonds that unite the entire Church to you. These can be broken neither by death nor by our apostolic power, according to canonical forms. Remain inviolably attached to them. Never abandon them in any way to the arbitrary will of rapacious wolves. Inflamed by a holy flame, you have raised your voice against a band of thieves. You have not wavered in going out to confront them with your legitimate authority.

We now address you, beloved sons, admirable canons of the chapters of France. You know how to obey your archbishops and bishops. You are united to your leaders. Together with them you form one ecclesial body and no civil power can dissolve you or subvert you. You have followed with honor in the footsteps of your illustrious prelates. You have set out on the right path and have not deviated from it. Never let any intruder, falsely dressed in the clothes of a bishop or his vicars, enter and take over the government of your churches. If they remain in the circumstances in which they are deprived of their pastors, their only remaining possibility to act will be based on what you speak to them when they are confronted with whatever new plots that some may try to concoct against you. Being of one heart and one mind, you are able to keep far away from you any kind of invasion or schism.

We turn to you, dear sons, pastors and auxiliary priests. Your number is great and your fortitude is constant. You are faithful in fulfilling your duties. You are very different from your colleagues who have succumbed to weakness, or have been seized by worldly ambition. They have sold themselves into slavery. We hope that they quickly heed our warnings and return to their rightful duties. Continue giving the good example that you have given to this point. Remember that only the legitimate can dare to give you the positions that you have been given. Even if the civil power prevents you from carrying out your responsibilities and chases you out of your parishes, you will be, nevertheless, the true pastors of the parish. You are still bound by your duties inasmuch as you are able, to catch the thieves who have forced their way into your place. They have no other goal than to ruin the salvation of the souls entrusted to you, souls for whom you well know that you will have to give an account to God.

We also wish to speak to you, beloved sons, priests and other ministers of the French Church. The Lord has called you to remain united to your legitimate pastors along with the Faith and the doctrine of the Church. You are obliged to do everything in your power to impede the sacrilegious usurpers and repel their advances.

We finally address you, our beloved children the Catholic faithful throughout France. We affectionately encourage you from the bottom of our heart to remember the Faith of your fathers. Never rebel from it because it is the True Religion that will lead you to Eternal Life. It gives life to civil society and enables it to flourish. Remain diligently on guard so that your ears might not fall prey to the seductive voices of the philosophy of this age. They will lead you to your death. They are all invaders, even if they call themselves archbishops, bishops, or pastors of parishes. Avoid them at all costs. Have nothing in common with them, above all in the exercise of religion. Be docile to the voices of your legitimate pastors who still live. Or, if they should die, those who are canonically installed after them. Listen to our voice as well. No one is able to be fully in the Church of Christ unless he is united to the visible head, which is established in the Chair of Peter. And so that you might be more eagerly dedicated to fulfilling your responsibilities, we have beseeched the Heavenly Father that he might grant you the spirit of counsel, truth, and constancy. We end by giving you, very dear sons and venerable brothers, as a sign of our paternal tenderness, our apostolic blessing.

Given at Rome from Saint Peter, 13 April 1791, the seventeenth year of our pontificate.

A Reminder to the bishop of Aleria and to the other bishops of Corsica
Pope Pius VI

To our venerable brother, Joseph, the bishop of Aleria: may God grant you salvation and we grant you our apostolic blessing.

The people of the island of Corsica, deceived by the wiles of some foreigners, have embraced the French Civil Constitution of the Clergy. The National Assembly passed this law. It is absolutely contrary to dogma, ancient discipline, and more recent discipline. Our paternal concern does not allow us to ignore you, our venerable brother, along with the chapters, priests, clergy and all of the faithful of your diocese. The duties of your office bind you tightly to us. We hope that you recognize this and that you do not wish to become schismatic, thus incurring the penalties imposed by the canons against those who corrupt doctrine and discipline. We clearly explained these duties at length in letters that we addressed to our sons, the Cardinals of the Holy Roman Church, to our venerable brothers the archbishops and bishops, to the chapters, priests, and faithful of the kingdom of France. We think it fitting to send you several copies of these letters, so that you and the faithful of your diocese might clearly know in the midst of the perturbations in which we find the Church. In addition, they will help you repel the sacrilegious efforts that wicked men have stirred up everywhere. These letters will support you in the midst of the terrible storm that violently rocks the boat of the Catholic Church. Once you are aware of these matters, your zeal and your eagerness for religion ought to grow greater. You will see how near are the dangers that threaten to wound the Church! In this hope, and led by our knowledge of your pastoral vigilance, we grant to you and to your flock our apostolic blessing.

Given at Rome, from Saint Peter, under the ring of the fisherman, 13 April 1791, the seventeenth year of our pontificate.